Lasting Relationship with God

By
Paul Gavaza, Ph.D

Second Edition

TEACH Services, Inc.
PUBLISHING
www.TEACHServices.com

World rights reserved. This book or any portion thereof may not be copied or reproduced in any form or manner whatever, except as provided by law, without the written permission of the publisher, except by a reviewer who may quote brief passages in a review.

This book was written to provide truthful information in regard to the subject matter covered. The author assumes full responsibility for the accuracy of all facts and quotations as cited in this book. The opinions expressed in this book are the author's personal views and interpretation of the Bible, Spirit of Prophecy, and/or contemporary authors and do not necessarily reflect those of TEACH Services, Inc.

This book is sold with the understanding that the publisher is not engaged in giving spiritual, legal, medical, or other professional advice. If authoritative advice is needed, the reader should seek the counsel of a competent professional.

First edition Copyright © 2007 by Paul Gavaza

Second edition Copyright © 2013 Paul Gavaza, Ph.D. & TEACH Services, Inc.

ISBN-13: 978-1-57258-901-8 (Paperback)
ISBN-13: 978-1-57258-903-2 (ePub)
ISBN-13: 978-1-57258-904-9 (Kindle/Mobi)

Library of Congress Control Number: 2012948885

Published by

TEACH Services, Inc.
P U B L I S H I N G
www.TEACHServices.com

All scripture quotations, unless otherwise indicated, are taken from the
Holy Bible, New International Version®, NIV®.
Copyright ©1973, 1978, 1984 by Biblica, Inc.™
Used by permission of Zondervan.
All rights reserved worldwide.

Scriptures quotations marked ESV are from *The Holy Bible*, English
Standard Version, copyright © 2001 by Crossway Bibles,
a division of Good News Publishers.
Used by permission. All rights reserved.

Bible texts credited to KJV are from the King James Version of the Bible.

Scripture quotations marked NKJV are taken from the New King James
Version®. Copyright © 1982 by Thomas Nelson, Inc.
Used by permission. All rights reserved.

All rights reserved. Bible texts credited to TEV are from
the *Good News Bible*—Old Testament: Copyright ©
American Bible Society 1976, 1992; New Testament:
Copyright © American Bible Society 1966, 1971, 1976, 1992.

Dedication

Dedicated to my sons Tatenda, and Takudzwa, and daughter Tafadzwa "Taffy" Gavaza

Table of Contents

Introduction 9

Chapter One
    God-Person Relationship 13

Chapter Two
    God-Person Relationship Marred By Sin 20

Chapter Three
    God Takes the Initiative 27

Chapter Four
    The Transformation Process 38

Chapter Five
    Reconciled With God 45

Chapter Six
    Christlike Character 53

Chapter Seven
    Learning Under the Master 62

Chapter Eight
    Working for the Master 69

Chapter Nine
> War With the Devil 77

Chapter Ten
> Christian Loyalty 82

Chapter Eleven
> Christian Suffering 88

Chapter Twelve
> Talking With God 98

Chapter Thirteen
> I Fall Yet I Rise Again 105

Chapter Fourteen
> Looking at the Prize 114

Introduction

The Scriptures describe humanity as "children," "sons" and "daughters" of God. This designation reveals both the experiences that God desires for His people and the central theme in God's grand plan to save humanity—a loving, trusting and lasting relationship between people and God. Originating from God, fine-tuning through life's phases and finally reaching consummation when the character fully reflects Christ's, the father–child relationship is a fitting symbol of God's eternal purpose and desire for the human race.

Just as the relationship between a child and his father develops over time until it becomes personal, trusting and intimate, so does the development in the relationship between people and God, as Christian characters approximate the full nature of Christ—the ideal. We develop Christlike characters as we maintain a lasting and trusting relationship with God. This process is a product of human efforts and God's grace whereby Christ's merits and his righteousness or perfection is imparted on the Christian. The divine act provides all people—you and me—with the moral perfection that we need in order to relate and associate with a perfect and righteous God.

As elaborated in the subsequent chapters, many people in the Scripture entered and maintained a lasting relationship with God. For example, Moses, Abraham, Joshua, Paul and Peter just to name a few cherished and nourished their personal relationship with God. Moses and Abraham had such a personal and close relationship with God that they were called friends of God (see Exod 33:11, James 2:23). In addition, the Bible says Enoch walked with God (see Gen 5:24) denoting the closeness and constance of his relationship with God. These people catalyzed the development of their relationship with God through the everyday choices they made. How is it with you? Do you personally have a relationship with God and are you happy with this relationship? Do you take time to nourish and develop this important relationship?

The quest for a lasting relationship with God is not limited to a day, a week, a month, or a year, but is a lifetime pursuit. To make Christ's life ours by faith is the supreme object of Christian life. God intends that His people, by developing a lasting relationship with Him, reflect the image of Jesus in their lives, having grown up into a perfect man or woman "to the measure of the stature of the fullness of Christ" (Eph. 4:13, NKJV). Christ desires to reproduce his character in all people and to restore the lost image of God in humanity. Godlikeness, or godliness, is the ideal for every child of God. The world awaits this unveiling and manifestation of God's character in His people. This is a 'work in progress' that continues as long as a person lives. God's purpose for humanity will be fully accomplished in the reward for the victors. Then, and only then, will the Christian experience have its final consummation wherein Christ's character is perfectly reproduced in His people. The human race will be restored to the trusting, loving, and lasting relationship with God.

The real test of true Christianity is in maintaining one's relationship with God in the midst of a sinful and changing world. *Lasting Relationship with God* is designed to offer guidance and devotional inspiration in the believer's quest for a unique, personal, loving, and lasting relationship with God. It will broaden and deepen the reader's appreciation of the need to develop a Christlike character and to nurture eternal fellowship with God. We will touch on various areas of a person's relationship with God, such as one's character, loyalty to God, suffering, struggle with evil, talking with God, and discipleship among others.

The various aspects of the Christian experience are presented in a simple and practical manner. How can sinners enter into a personal relationship with God? How can they cultivate, nourish, and develop this relationship? Can Christians be sure of their relationship with God whilst they still retain their self-centered nature and their character defects? Can we be effective in our discipleship and service for Christ when we are unsure of our relationship with God? This book seeks to answer these questions as we address two fundamental aspects of the Christian life: (a) becoming a Christian and (b) being a Christian. In the process we will learn about the active role of God in creating and sustaining the God–person relationship. Some biblical examples illuminate our journey of discovery and clarify the issues of a lasting relationship with God.

We explore the relationship between the development of a lasting, personal relationship between a person and God, character development, and the Christian's perfection and righteousness. It is my desire and prayer that as you read *Lasting Relationship with God*, you will be encouraged and motivated to make this experience yours through the choices you make today and to be fit for the life in heaven.

Your destiny depends on the preparation that you now make in developing your relationship with God. In the end God is not going to consider your job, bank account, political standing or status in church and society in deciding who to take to heaven. Instead, He will mainly consider your relation to (or posture toward) Christ. Christ is going to judge all people primarily by their accountability to God as reflected in their level of character development which is a mirror image of their relationship with Him. Irrespective of your background or your status in society, church, and home, you can have a positive and lasting relationship with God in this life and in the life to come. God wants to have a personal and rewarding relationship with you.

Paul Gavaza, PhD
September 2012

Chapter One

God-Person Relationship

Now this is eternal life: that they may know you, the only true God, and Jesus Christ, whom you have sent
—John 17:3

At Creation Adam and Eve, the holy pair, lived in bliss. They had around them everything lovely and attractive to enjoy. They had no cares and troubles that characterize our lives today. Notwithstanding, this is not what they valued or cherished most. Instead, what they prioritized above all other blessings was the company of God and the heavenly angels. They highly valued their cordial, perfect, and continuous relationship and association with God and holy angels. Adam and Eve were visited by angels and had open and joyful communion with their maker. At every visit Adam and Eve would have had much to say to the heavenly angels and God, excitedly relating the beauties of nature they had newly discovered in their lovely home.

From the very beginning, God made humans for relationships. Human beings were created to relate to God, to holy angels, and, above all, to relate to other humans and nature. In creating humankind, God set forth a process to initiate and develop a relationship between Himself and His people. Creation set in motion a complex network of relationships and interactions among numberless actors, both human and divine. Since the beginning God has been interested in establishing and maintaining a lasting and trusting relationship with all people.

One of the key elements we learn from the Creation account is that God is closely linked to the human family. Through Creation, God established a general relationship between the entire human race and Himself, as creature and Creator respectively. Human beings came from the hand of the Creator, God. They came from a royal line, the line of God. As a result of this link and relationship with God, they are entitled to the benefits and advantages that come with such a line. By virtue of His relationship with the human race and His gracious character, God is impelled to act in humankind's favour, though the latter may be sinners. People, as a result of this relationship with God, are assured of love, sympathy, and care from the all-powerful and omniscient God. God cares and provides for His people.

For Adam and Eve, the relationship went further to symbolize a father and child relationship. God was their father just as He is our father today.

The human person was created to be a practical being tasked with the practical job of being a steward. God conferred on Adam, and the entire human race, the responsibility to manage His "goods," which He had created. Men and women, as stewards, were given dominion over the whole earth (see Gen. 1:26). God made humanity ruler over everything that He had made. There was to be an intimate sharing between God, the owner, and humanity, the steward. He "put everything under his feet: all flocks and herds, and the beasts of the field, the birds of the air, and the fish of the sea, all that swim the paths of the sea" (Ps. 8:6–8). The human pair's stewardship of the things of God continually brought them into touch and communion with God. As good stewards, humanity enjoyed a positive and trusting relationship with their Maker, and other associated privileges and responsibilities.

In creating humans, God put in place two factors and conditions to facilitate and to promote the development of a lasting relationship between Himself and the human race; following is a discussion of these two factors:

Shared Characteristics and Attributes

God shared with human beings some of His own unique characteristics and attributes. To facilitate the development of a personal, trusting, and lasting relationship between Himself and the human race, God made human beings to be like Him. They were endowed with the very thoughts and feelings of God, as the former came from the hand of their Maker. God made human beings similar to Himself in at least two dimensions: in character and in perfection or righteousness. We discuss these in brief here:

Godlike Character

Human beings were created with the character akin to that of God. God fashioned Adam after His own character.

Adam and Eve were made in the image of God—formed in the likeness of God. Their traits of character were noble and untainted by sin. This element was important in order for people to be truly happy before God and to thereby relate cordially with Him.

Created Perfect and Righteous

The Bible says Adam and Eve were made in the image of God, and after His likeness (Gen. 1:26). They, like God, were perfect and righteous. God made the first human beings perfect in all their faculties; they had neither sin nor inclinations to sin. God made them holy and upright, to have no bias toward evil. At Creation, Adam and Eve did not know about evil, as they lived in a world that had not experienced sin and its consequences. In their Eden home, everything was perfect and beautiful. In this sinless state, the human pair, the supreme object of God's Creation, were to have a joyful communion with Him in whom "are hidden all the treasures of wisdom and knowledge" (Col. 2:3). In physical, mental, and spiritual nature, humanity bore a likeness to its Maker.

―⁂―

The likeness in attributes was designed and expected to facilitate and promote the development of a lasting relationship between people and God. It is not possible to have a perfect and lasting relationship with God when our characters are not godlike and when we are not righteous. A godlike character, with its attendant perfection and righteousness, is humanity's necessary prerequisite for beginning and maintaining a lasting relationship with God.

Interaction and Communion

In order to facilitate the development of a lasting relationship with the man and woman He created, God, from the outset, reached out to them through continuous interaction and communion. God occasionally descended to the garden to interact with the junior members of His kingdom, the human family. An environment of openness and mutuality existed. God talked to them and they talked to God without any barriers. Adam and Eve were visited by angels and were granted face-to-face communion with their Maker, with no obscuring veil between. In the process, the holy pair received instructions from God and learned more of Him, and thus their relationship with Him developed further.

God has always wanted to be in constant and eternal touch with His creatures. To facilitate the continuous interaction, the communion and fellowship with the human race, God capped Creation by making humankind His temple. Through making human hearts His temple, He envisaged to stay in the people's minds all the time. He planned to share in their woes, their happiness, strife, and contention by dwelling continuously and perpetually in humanity. He was not interested in merely observing the events occurring in people's lives but expected to share with and be part of them on a daily basis. Humanity is the temple of God, and He desires to build and beautify in every man a character in the image of divine perfection.

The human heart at Creation was truly noble and filled with the essence of heaven, which made it easy and possible for humans to relate with God. God was enthroned within the human heart as the divine source and origin of every impulse of life; every thought and feeling; and every word and deed. People's hearts and minds were inhabited and governed by God and driven by His Spirit.

Adam and Eve, as a result of these conditions and factors, enjoyed a positive and lasting relationship with God. The conditions and factors were solid bases and springboards for the development of the lasting relationship between God and people.

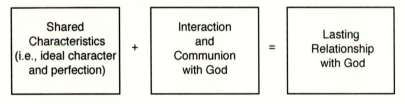

Human beings, in a lasting relationship with God, naturally had and enjoyed fellowship with God. The existence of the perfect and lasting relationship between God and humans allows for fellowship between humans and God. It is this fellowship built on the existence of a trusting and lasting relationship that God desired to have with all people in the world.

Fellowship, interaction and communion with God was the medium through which men and women were to develop and grow, and receive wisdom. By beholding God,

Adam and Eve became like Him. Similarly, we partake of His holiness and become sanctified as we commune with Him, too. People can attain His righteousness and His character through Christ (see John 15:5). There is no limit to the possibilities of a person's development if he or she is linked and connected to God. By maintaining a lasting relationship with God, Adam and Eve strategically placed themselves in the channel through which God's blessings flow. Similarly, when we are in a right relationship with God, we get all the blessings we need. The key is to have a right relationship with God.

From His experiences and dealings with holy angels, the perfect family in Eden, down to the patriarchs, prophets, and kings, to the time of Jesus Christ (on earth), and all the way down to our own time, God has emerged unequivocally as a God of relationships. He has demonstrated a special interest in creating and staying in a lasting relationship with the human race. God certainly wants you and me to know, in a profound and personal way, that we belong to Him and that nothing can change God's love for the human race. The connection between God and His people is close and decided. The sum and substance of Christian experience is matrixed on entering and maintaining a lasting relationship with God.

Chapter Two

God-Person Relationship Marred By Sin

The earth is now marred and defiled by sin
—Ellen G. White

Nature's harmony and perfection and the harmonious relationship between humankind and God was disturbed by sin. Sin was introduced in heaven by God's high-ranking angel named Lucifer. Lucifer, like all other angels and the rest of the world, was created perfect and blameless until iniquity was found in his heart. Scriptures record that Lucifer became proud, cherished hatred and jealousy in his heart, which led him to rebel against God (see Ezek. 28:12–19; Isa. 14:12–15).

Lucifer's sin introduced war and contention in the heavenly courts. Instead of viewing God as their father, friend, God, and King, Lucifer and his followers began to view Him as an enemy and foe. They stood before Him as rebels and dissidents where they once stood as trusted officers and children. They could no longer enjoy holiness nor could they take pleasure in associating with the Holy One. Satan and his angels thus lost the communion and fellowship they once enjoyed as perfect angels with God. As they insisted on their path of rebellion, they forfeited their place in heaven. They were cast down to the earth as enemies of God.

Hurled down to the earth and banished from God's presence, the devil deceived the human race to sin against God by eating the forbidden fruit. In the process, Satan and his agents introduced sin to our world (see Rom. 5:12) and thus broke the provision of eternal happiness and the continued existence of the positive and cordial relationship between God and humanity. Adam and Eve could obey and live, or disobey and perish, and they chose to disobey.

What is sin?

Sin is "the transgression of the law" (1 John 3:4, KJV), an act of crookedness and perverse behavior. It is a person's refusal to acknowledge God's authority in his or her life. Sin causes people to claim independence apart from God and to deny His right to command. Rightly understood as rebellion against God, the concept of sin refers to people's relationship with God. It defines a spoiled and fractured relationship between people and God. The real essence and problem of sin is in the separation it brings to the sinner from God. More importantly, as Fred L. Fisher says in his book *Falling Walls: The Doctrine of Reconciliation*, sin "is a matter of the being of man, not of his actions.... It [sin] is antagonism to the will of God.... It is in fact godlessness."[1] Sin is a state of being; it naturally and inevitably results in sinful thoughts and actions.

Sin makes people enemies of God. Sinners, being separate from God, are hostile to Him. Bible writers paint a gloomy picture of people living in sin. Paul used words such as "separate," "without hope," and "without God" to describe the condition of humans living in sin. For example, he says: "Remember that at that time you were separate from Christ, excluded from citizenship in Israel and foreigners to the covenants of the promise, without hope and without God in the world" (Eph. 2:12). In other passages he describes people as "enemies" of God (Rom. 5:10), "far off" (Eph. 2:13, NKJV), "hostile to God" (Rom. 8:7); they "cannot please God" (Rom. 8:8), are "separated from the life of God" (Eph. 4:18), stand under the "wrath of God" (Rom. 1:18), and are "condemned already" (John 3:18).[2]

These words and phrases depict a fractured relationship between people and God and portray a dark picture of their existence without God.

Adam and Eve's response to God's visit epitomizes the effect of sin on people's relationship with God. After Adam and Eve ate of the forbidden tree, they were no longer able and willing to associate with God as they were before. As God was coming to the Garden to visit and commune with the pair,

> Then the man and his wife heard the sound of the Lord God as He was walking in the garden in the cool of the day, and they hid from the Lord God among the trees of the garden. But the Lord God called to the man, "Where

are you?" He answered, "I heard you in the garden, and I was afraid because I was naked; so I hid" (Gen. 3:8–10).

After their sin, Adam and Eve could no longer find joy in holiness and in associating with a holy God. They rejected His friendship; their running away from God was evidence that they had severed their relationship with Him. Instead of welcoming their Creator and God as before, they were afraid and sought to hide from His presence. Today sin has the same effect on people. Sinners are alienated from God (see Isa. 59:2) and cannot be happy in God's presence.

All people, in their natural state, are enemies of God and cannot cordially and positively relate to God. The thoughts, interests, and motives of sinners are alien to those of God. The apostle Paul wrote: "The man without the Spirit does not accept the things that come from the spirit of God, for they are foolishness to him, and he cannot understand them, because they are spiritually discerned" (1 Cor. 2:14). Even if an amnesty could be done allowing sinners to enter heaven, they would shrink from the companionship of holy beings there. According to Ellen White, "Could he [the sinner] be permitted to enter heaven, it would have no joy for him.... Heaven would be to him a place of torture; he would long to be hidden from Him who is its light, and the center of its joy" (*Steps to Christ*, p. 17, 18).

Satan, in introducing sin, succeeded in souring people's relationship with God. In the process, Satan misrepresented God's character as being hard, demanding, tough, severe, and unforgiving. This destroyed the basis of our relationship with God. God's character was tarnished and continues to be tarnished by sin.

> ### How Many Are Sinners?
> Since its introduction, sin has spread to all humankind (see Rom. 3:23) and has grown in complexity. None among the human race is immune to sin. As a consequence, "there is no one righteous, not even one; there is no one who understands, no one who seeks God. All have turned away, they have together become worthless; there is no one who does good, not even one" (Rom. 3:10–12). According to the wise man, no one can say "I have kept my heart pure; I am clean and without sin" (Prov. 20:9). Evil has become a science, and vice is consecrated as though it were a part of religion. Our cities and towns continually conform to sin and moral decadence.

Sin is a tremendous evil. It not only alienates us from God but also perverts and corrupts human nature. Not only are people's outward acts wrong but also the very nature of people and their actions is morally perverse and distorted. Even before we start to act, talk, or walk, we are sinful and unholy, naturally. According to the psalmist, "Even from birth the wicked go astray; from the womb they are wayward and speak lies" (Ps. 58:3). He adds, "Surely I was sinful at birth, sinful from the time my mother conceived me" (Ps. 51:5). A corrupt environment may indeed socialize people into a culture of sin, but it easily does so because people are sinners by nature. Describing human nature, Bible writers penned:

"Your whole head is injured, your whole heart afflicted. From the sole of your foot to the top of your head there is no soundness—only wounds and bruises and open sores" (Isa. 1:5, 6); "The heart is deceitful above all things and beyond cure. Who can understand it?" (Jer. 17:9). Our hearts (minds), which are the source of all impulses, are in a terrible condition. The mind is carnal and cherishes sin all the time.

From the sinful nature prompted by the deceitful heart, people bring forth evil works that commensurate with their internal condition, thereby continually worsening their evil condition. People are unable to avoid sin even when their will is in the right place (see Rom. 7:15–19). As a result of their affected internal situation, human beings nurture a perpetual tendency toward sin rather than righteousness or goodness. They find joy in sin rather than in the presence of God, making it difficult to develop or maintain a positive relationship with God. Sadly, they seek to avoid rather than approach God. The result is deterioration or destruction of their relationship with Him. People cannot have fellowship with God whilst constantly going against His character.

> Fractured Relationship ⟶ No Fellowship between people and God

More importantly, our perverted nature means that we are unable to form righteous characters on our own. All people are powerless to escape the trap of sin. The Bible says, "Can the Ethiopian change his skin or the leopard its spots? Neither can you do good who are accustomed to doing evil" (Jer. 13:23). The human race can do nothing good that will commend them to God on their own. Ellen White penned, "All the culture and education which the world can give will fail of making a degraded child of sin a child of heaven.... Man cannot transform himself by the exercise of his will. He possesses no power by which this change can be effected" (*Christ's Object Lessons*, p. 96). There is nothing that humans can do to restore this broken relationship on their own. One author likened the severed relationship to a tree cut off from its roots or a branch severed from the vine. The tree, or the branch, can of itself do nothing to restore the situation.

The sin-caused separation between God and humanity comes with dire consequences. When we choose sin, we separate ourselves from the only source of our existence, sustenance, and purpose. If we are not connected to Christ, we are dead even though we may be biologically, emotionally, and intellectually sound. God is the fountain of life. Only as we maintain a lasting relationship with God do we enjoy the promise of one of the essential characteristics of God: eternal life.

No one can be truly happy when estranged from God. Whatever the outward appearance may deceptively suggest, there is no joy in the path that leads away from God's will and presence. Every person living in sin is devoid of the peace, joy, and blessings that come only with a positive and lasting relationship with God.

---

1   Fred L. Fisher, *Falling Walls: The Doctrine of Reconciliation* (Nashville: Convention Press, 1973), p. 20.

2   Fisher, *ibid.*, p. 18.

Chapter Three

God Takes the Initiative

God was reconciling the world to himself in Christ
—2 Corinthians 5:19

When the first man and woman sinned in the beginning, something external was needed to restore the harmony and friendship between humanity and God because, as highlighted in Chapter 2, on its own, humanity is characteristically incapable of restoring that right relationship with God. The Bible refers to this restoration of the right relationship between us and God as *reconciliation*.

> ## What is Reconciliation?
> To *reconcile* is to *restore to harmony or friendship.* According to the *Webster's New World Dictionary of the American Language* (1966), the word reconciliation is used in four ways: (1) to make friendly again or win over to a friendly attitude; (2) to settle or compose a quarrel or difference; (3) to make such things as arguments, ideas, or texts compatible or consistent; and (4) to make content or submissive. According to Fisher, "Reconciliation means the restoration of the forgiven sinner to the favor and
> *(cont.)*

> fellowship of God."[3] Reconciliation depicts a positive change in people's relationship and standing with God, for example from antagonism to harmony.

The use of the term *reconciliation* has been restricted to people's *relationship* to God, whether individually or as groups. In religious circles the concept of reconciliation has two components: (1) God's role in sending His Son to die on the cross, and (2) the conversion of an individual, which is the individual's response to that gift of salvation. This chapter discusses the first part, and the next chapter the second component of reconciliation.

When humanity sinned and became estranged from God, they needed someone to lift them because they could not lift themselves up to God. Like the lost sheep, the soul that has wandered away from God is helpless, and unless divine love comes to its rescue, it can never find its way back. God's response package came through the plan of redemption. God's plan to send His Son was not an afterthought; the Bible teaches that it was before the foundation of the earth that God established a plan as a contingency measure in case humans sinned (see Rev. 13:8, KJV). Even before the first humans sinned, God had put in place a solution by which He could restore the broken relationship and destroy the barriers that people, through sin, might create.

Many Bible passages portray God as not just the principal actor in people's reconciliation to God but, more importantly, as its initiator. The restoration of the harmony and friendship between a person and God does not come through that person's own seeking after God but rather through God's seeking after him or her. An individual is acted upon by divine intervention. God conceived, designed, and implemented a plan to restore the right relationship between human beings and Himself.

When Adam and Eve sinned, God immediately put into action His plan that would involve His Son dying for sinful humanity. Paul wrote: "When the time had fully come, God sent his Son, born of a woman, born under law, to redeem those under law, that we might receive the full rights of sons" (Gal. 4:4, 5). God did not wait for His people to reconcile themselves to Him; He offered them redemption and restoration. Through Christ, God reconciled Himself with them. Christ identified Himself with the needs and interests of humanity. To the Corinthians and the Romans, Paul wrote, "God was reconciling the world to himself in Christ" (2 Cor. 5:19); "when we were God's enemies, we were reconciled to him through the death of his Son" (Rom. 5:10). Reconciliation was inconceivable without the incarnation.

Here is revealed the paradox of paradoxes! God, the aggrieved, instead of holding human beings accountable for their transgression and rebellion as they deserved and banishing them from the face of the earth, took steps toward restoring the broken relationship by offering His son to die in their place. When the time came, Jesus died for all sinners, even the worst of sinners—including those who persecuted and killed him. Much more fascinating is that God did all this while people "were still sinners"

(Rom. 5:8) who did not acknowledge or consider the evil they had done.

What Prompted this Action?

Certainly God's great love for the human race played a big part in the paradox. Notwithstanding the gloomy situation the human race found itself in, God still loved the entire human race. In John 3:16 we read that it was because God loved the world so much that He gave His only Son. He loved the sinful world so much that he provided the propitiation. The parable of the prodigal son teaches that God does not forsake those who choose to stray from Him (see Luke 15:11–32). God's love for the human race is unconditional. This is grace. Christ loves guilty and helpless sinners, and His hand is outstretched toward those who err. God loves the human race to the extent that He yearns over one who chooses to sin. His love is without parallel. Human language is unable to accurately describe the height, depth, and breadth of God's love for the human race.

> **Grace**
>
> Ellen White defined God's grace as an attribute of God exercised toward undeserving human beings. Grace is God's unmerited favor and His giving of good things or blessings we do not deserve. According to Mary Fairchild, "Grace is divine assistance given to humans for their regeneration (rebirth) or sanctification; a virtue coming from God; a state of sanctification enjoyed through divine favor."[4]
>
> *(cont.)*

God Takes the Initiative

> God is gracious and rejoices in bestowing His blessings or favors upon His people, not because they are worthy, but notwithstanding their unworthiness. Their only claim to His mercy is their great need. God's grace cannot be earned; it is a gift of God (see Eph. 2:8). Grace is all-inclusive, abundant, and unlimited, and it extends to all people. Grace is possible because of Christ's death.

God's estimation of humanity's worth drove Him to initiate reconciliation. Even sinful human beings are of inextricable value to their Creator. Jesus in the parable of the lost coin teaches that just like "the coin, though lying among dust and rubbish, is a piece of silver still. Its owner seeks it because it is of value. So every soul, however degraded by sin, is in God's sight accounted precious" (*Christ's Object Lessons*, p. 194). The value of the human race to God stems from Creation and also from redemption. The intrinsic value of humankind is not the major issue; it is the value placed upon it by the loving master. God gives human beings value beyond the realm of human computation or conception. Even though you may be living in sin, you are distinctively valuable in God's sight.

As a perfect representative of the Father, Christ was prompted to reconcile humanity in order to portray to the world an accurate picture of God and thus vindicate God as a God of love. Jesus, by dwelling among people, revealed to the world and to angels the true character and nature of God, which is in complete contrast to the character of Satan. God, who had been accused as being a tyrant and a dictator, was painted in the mission of

Jesus as a friend of the human race, someone who seeks people's good and not their ruin. Thus, through Christ's redeeming work, the government of God stands justified. The Omnipotent One is made known as the God of love, full of compassion, mercy, and tenderness.

What Did the Work of Christ Achieve?

The incarnation of Jesus was targeted primarily toward the restoration of the right relationship between God and human beings. The work of Christ achieved this through linking human beings and God, demonstrating to them how to live in a right relationship with God and, most importantly, through vanquishing sin and Satan.

Christ's Mission Linked Humanity With God

The mission of Christ linked heaven and earth and reversed the separation that sin had wrought on humankind's relationship with God. It facilitated the supreme fusion between divinity and humanity. Christ, by his life and death, provided the way to God. He said, "I am the way and the truth and the life. No one comes to the Father except through me" (John 14:6). By his humanity Christ touched humanity; by his divinity he lays hold upon the throne of God. Through Christ, the sin-induced gulf between God and human beings is bridged.

Through the incarnation, Christ permanently united himself with humanity. It is by virtue of this union and bond that people are restored to a cordial relationship with

God. By assuming human nature, Christ elevated humanity. Fallen people are placed where, through connection with Christ, they may indeed become worthy of the name "sons of God" (see Rom. 8:19, 9:26; Gal. 3:26). Due to the work of Christ, people are closely united to God.

Christ's Mission Demonstrated How to Live in a Right Relationship With God

Jesus came to earth not only to make atonement for sin but through his life to demonstrate to the sinful and perishing world how to live in a right relationship with God. He lived a righteous life, thereby leaving humanity an example to follow. The Bible says, "Whoever claims to live in him must walk as Jesus did" (1 John 2:6). The life of Christ was characterized by humility (see Phil. 2:6–8), dependence upon God (see John 5:19, 30), a determination to do only the Father's will (see John 6:30, 38), thoughtfulness of others (see Acts 10:38), and a willingness to sacrifice and suffer, and even to die, for the good of others (see 2 Cor. 8:9; Rom. 5:6–8; 1 Pet. 2:24). Jesus lived a sinless life, and in Him no guile was found. He lived a life of obedience to the will of God. The followers of Christ should have the same mind that was in Christ (see Phil. 2:5). As Son of man, He gave us an example of obedience.

Christ's Mission Vanquished Sin and Satan

Jesus, through His life and death, conquered sin, death, and Satan, most importantly. It was Christ's mission first to conquer the ruler of this world and to establish Himself as the rightful king of humanity and the earth. Christ vanquished the power of sin. The very core of our Lord's mission was to rescue people from the bondage of sin. Jesus' blood paid the price for people's sins. Christ bore people's sins and died as their sacrifice. "Christ was treated as we deserve, that we might be treated as He deserves. What an unbelievable exchange! He was condemned for our sins, in which He had no share, that we might be justified by His righteousness, in which we had no share. He suffered the death, which was ours, that we might receive the life, which was His" (*The Desire of Ages*, p. 25).

Jesus Christ's mission on earth established a new and better covenant relationship between God and all people (see Heb. 8:6). The new covenant is not written in tablets of stone but in the hearts of individuals, as prophesied by the prophet Jeremiah (see Jer. 31:31). The new covenant relationship was inaugurated by His sacrificial blood (see Matt. 26:28; Luke 22:20; 1 Cor. 11: 25).

God Made Covenants With Man

God made covenants when He established relationships with the human race. A covenant is an agreement made to regulate relationships between two unequal parties (God and humans), involving obligations and promises. It is a compact entered into by two parties, with engagements on both sides, and ratified in solemn form. A covenant signifies the existence of a relationship. God made covenants with Noah (see Gen. 6:18), the patriarchs (see Gen. 15:18; Rom. 11:27), Israel (see Exod. 24), and David (see 2 Sam. 7). Covenants were sealed with the blood of sacrifice (see Exod. 24:8; Zech. 9:11) prior to the death of Jesus (NIV Bible index).

When God enters into a covenant relationship with His creatures, He binds Himself. Because God suffers Himself to contract certain duties to men and women, it gives them rights. Had God not made such provisions and taken such risks, His creatures would have no rights, for they can enjoy no good but such as He gives.

This new covenant relationship established a new religion—introduced Christianity. This covenant relationship is more than a religious profession. Its heart is not an ideal, a philosophy, even a lifestyle; it is a person—Jesus Christ. The essence of Christian life is to have and to maintain a trusting and loving relationship with Jesus. The real test of true Christianity is in maintaining one's relationship with God in the midst of a changing and sinful world.

Christianity

Most people view Christianity simply as a large world religion with many diverse groups. Christianity is more than an idea or a set of doctrines. It is a lifestyle that is characterized by a commitment to Jesus Christ and a close relationship between an individual and a person, Jesus Christ. Thus, Christianity rightly understood is not "primarily a matter of producing good deeds and eliminating wrong deeds from our lives through grit and determination. It is primarily a matter of entering and maintaining a relationship with Jesus in which we submit our wills to His." [5]

The ministry of Christ opened the way for fellowship between people and God. Scriptures teach that all people were reconciled with God through the life, mission, and death of Jesus. Paul wrote, "Now in Christ Jesus you who once were far away have been brought near through the blood of Christ" (Eph. 2:13). God, by sending His Son to die, achieved reconciliation for all humans potentially, and for the believer actually, in his or her personal experience of faith. Through the ministry of Christ, the cordial relationship between God and humanity can once again be restored. The plan of salvation foregrounded divinity's endeavour to elevate humankind to lofty heights of a fulfilling life worth living.

Divine agencies are moving upon the hearts of people, inviting them to have a lasting relationship with God. In Matthew 11:28, 29, Jesus says, "Come to me, all you who are weary and burdened, and I will give you rest. Take my yoke upon you and learn from me, for I am gentle and humble in heart, and you will find rest for your souls."

The call and invitation is open and glaring. The invitation has no barriers with respect to race, creed, and culture but transcends all boundaries. Whosoever is interested may be reconciled to God. Jesus is going from person to person, through influences seen and unseen, in a bid to attract you to a saving relationship with Him. He is standing in front of your soul temple, proclaiming, "I stand at the door and knock" (Rev. 3:20). Will you open your heart's door to the heavenly King?

In conclusion, given that sinners are unable to restore themselves to a right relationship with God, only God could remedy the situation. God took the initiative by conceiving, designing, and implementing a plan to restore humanity to a right relationship with Him. The plan involved the life and death of his only beloved Son, Jesus Christ. Jesus assumed human nature, then suffered and died for you in order to reconcile you with God. Through His own initiative, God brought Himself within the reach of man. What God has done and is doing, however, is but only half the story. As the following chapter elaborates, restoring the right relationship between us and God requires that we also play a part.

---

3 Fisher, *ibid.*, p. 12

4 Mary Fairchild, "Grace," About.com Christianity, http://christianity.about.com/od/glossary/g/grace.htm (accessed August 27, 2012).

5 Robert S. Folkenberg, *We Still Believe*, (Nampa, ID: Pacific Press, 1994), p. 28.

Chapter Four

The Transformation Process

The Lord is not slack concerning His promises ...but is longsuffering to us-ward, not willing that any should perish, but that all should come to repentance
—2 Peter 3:9, KJV

During Pentecost many were so convicted of their sins that they asked, "What shall we do?" Peter's first word in his response was "Repent" (Acts 2:38). When people realize their guilt, repentance offers the way of escape. The sinner may take the first step toward having a cordial and lasting relationship with God through repentance. It is the very first step that all who would return to God must take.

Repentance is the path sinners take back to God. There is no other way available to humankind. Jesus said, "Unless you repent, you too will all perish" (Luke 13:3). It is that simple; repent or perish.

Just like the leaven—something added wholly from outside—must be put into the meal before the desired change can be wrought, so the sinner must receive the grace of God before he or she can be fit for the kingdom of God. The wooing and drawing of the Spirit of God commence the process of repentance.

The Transformation Process

Genuine repentance is implanted in the heart through an understanding of the love of God in giving Christ to the world. As man beholds and comprehend the infinite sacrifice offered by the Son of God on their behalf, their hearts are softened and they long to be cleansed, and to be restored to communion with heaven. As we take time to "behold the Lamb of God, which taketh away the sin of the world" (John 1:29) we are led to repentance. [6]

What is Repentance?

Repentance is a sorrow for sin. Repentance is the way back to Christ. Robert H. Pierson explains that the Latin term from which our English word *repent* comes means "to creep back." [7] And that is just what true repentance means: "to creep back." This involves a change of mind, or a turning away from sin. *Repentance* also involves thinking and acting differently in one's life. *Repentance* entails a change of direction; thus, instead of doing what you please, you turn around and start doing what pleases Christ.

We truly repent when we decidedly turn away from wrongdoing. This is more than just feeling bad for our previous misdeeds or wrongdoings. True repentance acknowledges the wrongdoing, accepts Jesus' forgiveness and His cleansing and does not presume on the grace of God. It does not make excuses for sin.

True repentance is clearly seen in David's plea for mercy after his moral fall, as recorded in Psalm 51:

> Have mercy upon me, O God, according to your unfailing love; according to your great compassion blot out my transgressions. Wash away my iniquity and cleanse me from my sin. For I know my transgressions, and my sin is always before me. Against you, you only, have I sinned and done what is evil in your sight, so that you are proved right when you speak and justified when you judge. (verses 1–4)

"There is in this cry no excuse, no apology, no attempt to vindicate, no complaint against the justice of the law that condemned him. In true humility David blames no one but himself" (*The SDA Bible Commentary*, vol. 3, p. 755). David's repentance was not motivated by fear of the consequences of his actions. His repentance was sincere, honest and personal. He made no attempt to minimize the enormity of his sin. David appreciated the enormity of his transgression against God and he hated his sin. This is the repentance required to restore your right relationship with God.

Reactions to Guilt

Two rather different reactions to one's guilt are portrayed in Scripture in the examples of Judas and Peter. Even though Peter at one time declared emphatically, "even if I had to die with you, I will never disown you" (Mark 14:31), he, however, did deny Jesus when Jesus was on trial. However, after denying his master, Peter

(cont.)

> went away not to hang himself as Judas did, but to weep in repentance, thus once again restoring his relationship with Jesus.

The recognition of one's sin is important and necessary for repentance. Sensing our need, recognizing our poverty and sin, is the very first condition of acceptance with God. Only people who have an accurate estimation of their sinfulness will be able to renounce their sins. We must understand our danger, or we shall not flee to the refuge. We must feel the pain of our sinful condition, or we should not seek respite. Those who are whole do not need a physician (Luke 5: 31). It is only those who know themselves to be sinners that Christ can save. He came to "proclaim freedom for prisoners and recovery of sight for the blind, to release the oppressed" (Luke 4:18).

As previously noted, all people are sin-sick and are in need of cure (of a doctor). When we perceive ourselves as we truly are, we should come to Christ for forgiveness. The recognition of our need and poverty caused by sin is possible, as the Holy Spirit convicts us of sins we have committed.

Repentance is change. Change is part of life and is necessary in both the spiritual and in the natural world. The premise of spiritual life is change, and the spiritual life is to be viewed as a conscious process of progressive change.

> ## What Must Change?
> Our problems stem from the spiritual condition of our hearts. Thus, the change required to bring us into harmony with God should be of the heart. "There are many who try to reform by correcting this and that bad habit, and they hope in this way to become Christians, but they are beginning in the wrong place. Our first work is with the heart" (*Christ's Object Lessons*, p. 97). It is people's hearts that change in the process of repentance. Focus on preparing your heart so that God can work on it.

Repentance involves turning your heart to God, drawing near to Him, and feeding on Him. It involves turning the affections of our hearts toward God and having faith in His grace.

Although repentance is our first step, it does not end at the beginning of our relationship with God. Repentance recurs throughout the entire Christian experience. The Christian experience is characterized by ever-deepening repentance. We are to continually and constantly die to self and become more alive to God. As we get closer and nearer to Christ, we will see more clearly our deficiencies (some we never noticed before) and deformities of character that ought to be put away through repentance. We enter the Lord's unique life-changing program the day we receive Christ, and that program continues for life.

> ## Repentance Has a Cost
> Repentance is a costly venture and painful process. It requires determined, earnest effort and diligent labor. Anyone who
> *(cont.)*

The Transformation Process

> wishes to be a friend of God must of consequence give up the world and everything in it. This may include giving one's resources, talents, desires, hobbies, ambitions, life, and, most importantly, cherished sins. People cannot continue to develop a lasting relationship with Him while at the same time clinging to their sins or their old ways of life. These must be given up. We must be willing to sacrifice all for the new relationship with God. We must be able to say as Paul did, "I do not count my life of any value nor as precious to myself" (Acts 20:24).

It is important to note that there are obstacles to repentance. When sinners seek to return to God, they will encounter criticism, distrust, and seemingly insurmountable obstacles, all calculated by the devil to discourage and keep them away from God. Notwithstanding the cost involved, they can indeed make the necessary change. It is within the reach of all people. The Bible is emphatic about this. No person is too sinful, degraded, or wasted for the power of God. God has always been and is still in the rehabilitation business—bringing about personal change in people's lives.

Every individual on earth must arrive at a crucial decision. The choice is between repenting and not repenting. It is a big mistake to put off the work of repentance, even for a short time. You need not wait to make yourself better first; you are to come to Christ just as you are. It does not matter how messy your life is or how terrible the feelings are that you have been harboring toward God. It does not matter how remote or near God seems. It does not matter how successful your life may seem or actually be. You ought to come to Christ through repentance just as you are, with all your sins, weaknesses, and fears, and hand over the whole load to Christ.

As Christ stands at the door of your life knocking, attracting your mind away from sin to a positive relationship with Him, will you yield? Won't you by God's grace take time to behold the Saviour who loved you so much to the point of dying for you? Won't you heed His persistent knock at the door of your heart? He is seeking to draw you to Himself through repentance. He longs for you to respond. He is ready to restore you to a positive relationship with Himself, to give you a new life and a new beginning. Take the assertive steps toward repentance. If you have not done so before, I invite you to repeat the following short prayer:

Dear Lord Jesus, thank you for dying on the cross for my sins. I accept you as my Lord and Savior. Please forgive my sins and give me the gift of eternal life. I want to do your will in my life. Amen.

I believe that if you prayed this prayer, you have been ushered into the kingdom of God and you are now reconciled with God.

---

6   Ty Forrest Gibson, *The Path of the Just* (Malo, WA.: Light Bearers, 1991), p. 24.

7   Robert H. Pierson, *Though The Winds Blow: A Daily Guide to Successful Living* (Nashville: Southerton, 1968).

Chapter Five

Reconciled With God

If anyone is in Christ, he is a new creation
—2 Corinthians 5:17

The love and grace God so freely extended to the human race achieves reconciliation between an individual and God when that individual accepts it through repentance. If your repentance is genuine, you will be restored to a cordial and lasting relationship with God. Reconciliation reverses the separation of a person from God as brought about by sin. This transformation is beyond the ability of mere human power to accomplish. It is a supernatural work that enables people once again to commune with Him in this life and in heaven.

The reconciled people become not only Christians but sons and daughters of God, his brothers and sisters, his friends. The reconciled people become like Him (see 1 John 4:17) and begin to enjoy a harmonious relationship with God. The evidence of this new relationship is a transformed life.

The change that takes place in an individual involves four major steps and processes:
1. sins are forgiven,
2. righteousness is imputed,
3. a new creature is formed, and
4. a perfect relationship and fellowship with God are es-

tablished.

These four steps and stages, which are not necessarily mutually exclusive, are given and discussed below:

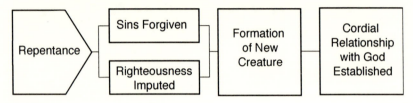

Sins Forgiven

If a person's repentance is genuine, he or she will receive forgiveness in return. When a person comes to Christ, He (Christ) does not condemn him but grants the sinner full and free forgiveness. There is a remission of sins that are past. The apostle John wrote, "If we confess our sins, He is faithful and just to forgive us our sins" (1 John 1:9). Moreover, Christ does more than just forgive sins; He takes away the sin (see Ps. 103:12; Mic. 7:19), and He will not remember them anymore (see Heb. 10:17). In the process, the sinner's standing and attitude toward and his or her relationship with the Lord are transformed.

Imputed Righteousness

The apostle John wrote that God not only forgives sinners who repent but also cleanses them from all unrighteousness (see 1 John 1:9) and they receive the declared righteousness of Christ (see Rom. 3:21–26). The sinner is imputed with Christ's righteousness. The sinner's past is covered with the righteousness of Christ, and God accounts him or her as righteous. God imparts His righteousness to the sinner.

New Creature Formed

When a person has been reconciled with God, he or she becomes a new creature, the Scriptures teach. The transformation that takes place in the Christian's life is not a modification or improvement of the old but a transformation of the nature. The old nature of sin dies, and the person becomes a new person altogether. Paul penned, "If anyone is in Christ, he is a new creation" (2 Cor. 5:17). A totally new being in the image of God is created. The new being will have a new moral state, a new moral power and, above all, a new heart in place of the old heart of stone. The new being will have a new spirit, God's Spirit, take possession of the heart (see Ezek. 36:26).

According to Fred Fisher, "Reconciliation so changes the whole being of man that he is no longer helpless, ungodly, a sinner, and at enmity with God; he is now at peace with God, has an entrance into His grace, is assured of continued salvation, and the love of God has become a dynamic reality in his life."[8] A transformation will be evident in the character (i.e., the tendency of the habitual words and acts). The difference between what a sinner was and what he or she becomes will be marked, deep, complete, and abiding.

Ellen White adds: "The things they once hated they now love, and the things they once loved they hate. The proud and self-assertive become meek and lowly in heart.

The vain and supercilious become serious and unobstructive ...duty becomes a delight, and sacrifice a pleasure" (*Steps to Christ*, pp. 48, 49). When the Spirit of God takes possession of the heart, love, humility, and peace take the place of anger, envy, and strife.

Christ Himself abides in the new person (see Gal. 2:20). When Christ abides in the heart through His spirit, He conforms the purposes, thoughts, feelings, and actions to the will of God.

These changes in a Christian mark the beginning of the development of a positive and lasting relationship with God, which is characterized by an earnest desire to please God and to have fellowship with others.

The Scriptures portray, in varied ways, the nature and type of relationship that begins and develops between God and a person who is reconciled with Him. Below we briefly discuss some of the God–person relationships as portrayed in Scripture, knowing that even these fall short of accurately describing the scope and intimacy of the relationship between God and His people. Human language is altogether feeble in describing the real relationship that exists and should exist between God and His people.

Father–Child Relationship

The psalmist, likening the relationship between a repentant man and God to that between a father and his children, wrote, "As a father has compassion on his children, so the Lord has compassion on those who fear him" (Ps. 103:13). Those who are reconciled with God are regarded as members of the heavenly family. People, upon reconciliation with God, become sons and daughters of God. The Scriptures, both in the New and Old Testaments, describe God as the Father of the repented human race (see John 1:12, 13, 2 Thess 1:1, Matt 6:9).

Those reconciled with God enjoy the same father–child relationship that Adam and Eve enjoyed prior to the fall. God becomes their Father. Through reconciliation we are once again accepted before God as trusted children, sons and daughters. Jesus said: "Yet to all who received him, to those who believed in his name, he gave the right to become children of God—children born not of natural descent, nor of human decision or a husband's will, but born of God" (John 1:12, 13).

As the relationship between human fathers and sons is intimate, personal, certain, so is the relationship between the reconciled people and God. Jesus, teaching his followers to pray, said, "This, then, is how you should pray: 'Our Father in heaven.'" (Matt. 6:9). Addressing God as "our Father" gives assurance and a deep personal conviction that we are His children and that He is our Father. There is no greater honor and privilege bestowed on human beings than to address God as their father or daddy.

Brother–Brother/Sister Relationship

Jesus is also linked to the human race as a brother. Paul wrote that "Jesus is not ashamed to call them brothers" (Heb. 2:11). Christ is not remote from you and me; He is a brother to the human race. Referring to the human race, Paul wrote that Jesus had to be made like his brothers (see Heb. 2:17). Jesus Himself said, "Here are my brothers! For whoever does the will of My father in heaven is my brother and sister and mother" (Matt. 12:49, 50). When we are reconciled with God, He (Christ) becomes our brother and we become members of His family.

Friend–Friend Relationship

Jesus calls His followers "friends" (John 15:15). Abraham and Moses were called "friends" of God (see Exod. 33:11; James 2:23).

The old hymn by Joseph M. Scriven, "What a Friend We Have in Jesus" talks of our loving and faithful Savior as one who wants to be your friend. A friend is someone who is available for you, accepts you, believes in you, forgives you, makes you laugh, and enjoys your company. This is what Jesus wants to be to you. He cares for you regardless of what you have done in the past. He offers unconditional love and is much closer than a sister, brother, or mother. The greatest treasure you can find is having Jesus as a friend. Jesus becomes your friend when you are reconciled with God.

If you are longing for companionship, Jesus is there for you. Do you need a friend? Consider Jesus! Jesus considers you His friend, and He longs to be friends with you, not just your acquaintance. God wants you to value

Him as a friend.

> **Jesus is my best friend.**
>
> I have not found a friend more trustworthy and reliable than Jesus. Jesus believes in me and accepts me regardless of what I have done and who I have been in my life. When I make a mistake or am selfish and unreasonable, He does not forsake me. I share with Him my deepest and darkest secrets. I can reach Him anytime I need Him, and He enjoys spending time with me. He cares about me, listens to me, understands me, and offers me unconditional love. I have found so much peace and security since I became His friend. I can say with certainty that Jesus is my best friend.

When we are reconciled with God, we indeed become His children (sons and daughters), brothers, sisters and friends. We are restored to the right, cordial, and trusting relationship with God that Adam and Eve enjoyed before the fall. We begin to see God not as harsh, severe, exacting, and hard but as someone to be loved, adored, and approached as a father, brother, and friend. God assures us of this relationship on many occasions. He wants you to appreciate this fundamental fact and enter into the most personal relationship you can ever have (see John 1:12; John 15:14).

When we repent or respond to Christ's call, it is just like a woman who says "I love you too" to a prospective groom. When a woman responds by saying "I love you too" to her prospective husband's move, it only signals the beginning of a relationship. They are not yet married, but they will have entered into and started a relationship. It is a relationship that could materialize into a wedding and a happy marriage on the one hand or that could break up after some point if one party proves unfaithful or both parties simply prove incompatible. The parties will have to develop their relationship over time until it becomes intimate and close. The started relationship will have its own experiences, challenges, pleasures, and lessons until marriage time and beyond. When people accept Christ, they go through a similar process. They will meet challenges, impediments, and joys as they develop their relationship with Him, who at a time in the future will come to take them home (to heaven). Christ has left His people with a promise, the promise of His soon return to take them and wed them. He now takes the time to look and test the sincerity of their love as it develops with each passing day.

---

8   Fisher, p. 12.

Chapter Six

Christlike Character

A noble character is earned by individual effort through the merits and grace of Christ—Ellen G. White

The majority of people in our world who start a relationship with God falter along the way. Like Balaam and Judas Iscariot, who also started a relationship with God, many fail to nurture and cultivate their relationship. In addition to starting a relationship with Him, God also desires that we nurture and cultivate the relationship. The relationship needs to be cherished, built, and nourished until it is fully developed, permanent, and personal. It must develop.

What is involved in that process? The process of developing one's relationship with God can be compared to mountain climbing. Mountain climbers start at the base of the mountain or slope, that is, at point A, and their goal will be to reach the top, point Z, as Figure 1 below depicts. At each stage of the climbing, the climbers get closer and closer to the top until they reach the top. The process of climbing itself is a struggle and involves hustling and bustling. Mountain climbers meet impediments in their quest to attain their goals.

Figure 1: *Stages of development in a person's relationship with God*

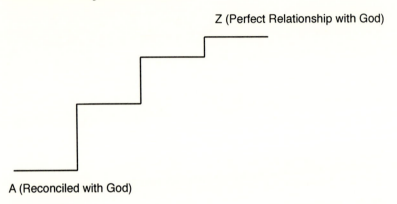

Noticeably, when people are reconciled with God, they start to climb the ladder of Christian growth until they achieve a perfect, cordial, and personal relationship with God. Christian life may be characterized as a move of faith from point A to point Z as Figure 1 demonstrates. As Christians move from point A to Z, their relationship with God becomes deeper and personal. As Christians move toward the mark, there will be a corresponding development in their perfection (righteousness) and character. No one whose character does not change or whose level of perfection is static can have a deeper, personal, and lasting relationship with God. These three variables vary positively and are discussed in turn below:

Relationship With God

The ultimate goal of reconciliation is to bring people to the right relationship with God, which Adam and Eve enjoyed at Creation. As noted in Chapter 1, humankind at Creation enjoyed a perfect, cordial, intimate, and lasting relationship with God. At the time people are reconciled with God, they do not immediately attain this goal. However sincere one's conversion may be, the person does not immediately attain a perfect, lasting, and personal relationship with God but begins the process toward that goal. A person's cordial relationship with God is restored at reconciliation, but due to a prior long attachment to sin, the relationship will not be perfect. The person *becomes* a Christian at conversion, but it does not end there; *becoming* a Christian means *beginning* a lifelong journey of growth in one's relationship with God.

Christian Perfection

People need perfection in order to associate or relate meaningfully with a perfect God. It is pretentious to expect to have a lasting relationship with God while still clinging to known sins. Followers of Christ are to be perfect in their lives as He was. God, on the merits of His Son, Jesus Christ, justifies (makes holy) the reconciled people. He makes them right with Himself. Perfection or righteousness with respect to the Christian life can be viewed in two ways.

Imputed Righteousness, or Relative Perfection

Imputed righteousness, or relative perfection, is the righteousness that God credits to sinners when they repent and are reconciled with God. God considers them perfect, or righteous. God does so by crediting to them, or imputing to them, the perfection and righteousness of Christ. It is a heavenly provision that allows sinners, not having their own righteousness but the imputed righteousness of Christ, to be complete in Christ. The merits of Christ stand in place of the sinner.

It is important to note here that God considers all honest Christians perfect at every stage of their development. They remain perfect in God's eyes as long as they obey all the light they receive. Christians, however, cannot be sinless, nor do they, in God's eyes, perfectly obey all of God's laws and satisfy all His requirements, but God regards them as if they never sinned. An individual may be a sinner because of the many things he or she may yet be ignorant of. However, the righteousness of Christ covers these character defects and sins. God overlooks (or "winks" at) our unintended ignorance (Acts 17:30).

This credited perfection describes all the levels beginning with A and then up the ladder but does not include Z in Figure 1, as long as people are striving toward a higher level of perfection during the course of their lives. This imputed perfection makes it possible for people such as the thief on the cross to be counted righteous despite having lived his life in sin and repented only a few minutes before his death.

Imparted Righteousness or Full Perfection

Imparted righteousness describes the Christian experience at its fully developed and completed stage. The people who reach this stage will be perfect and will be keeping all of God's commandments. They will have attained the sinless state in which Adam and Eve lived before their transgression. People will be holy, without blemish and without fault. At this stage the very image of God is reproduced in humanity. This is the destination of the entire Christian experience. This is the mark that all Christians press toward and is represented on the ladder as point Z. As people have a closer walk with God by developing their relationship with Him, they cumulatively become faultless in their deportment and in their attitude.

Character Development

The process of Christian growth and development as depicted in Figure 1 can also be viewed from the perspective of character development, against which the Christian experience is benchmarked. When a person is reconciled with God (i.e., at point A), the impress made by sin, the mind's propensity for evil, and, most of all, the deformities in the character will remain. As people receive and perceive divine light and redeeming grace, they will discern in themselves deformities of character they did not know were there. They will need to work on these character deformities and overcome them at each stage as their relationship with God develops. *Developing a lasting relationship with God is ultimately a process of character building. In developing and maintaining a relationship with God, people will be fine-tuning their characters in accordance with heavenly principles.*

The ideal model of Christian character is Christlikeness. Character development will continue until the Christian's character becomes Christlike (i.e., at point Z). A person at that stage will have grown up into a perfect man or woman, "to the measure of the stature of the fullness of Christ" (Eph. 4:13, NKJV). God Himself, in such a case, would be the ruler of one's life.

> ## Character Is Solemn
> Character development is a solemn responsibility and a special privilege. It is the most important duty given to humankind. Character building is a work of a lifetime. Throughout life people are expected to be working on their character defects to produce a Christlike character through the merits of Christ. The object of Christian life is to reproduce the character of Christ in the believer, that it may in turn be reproduced in others. Christ is seeking to reproduce Himself in the hearts of His people. God will not change the characters of people at His coming. How people build and develop their characters during their earthly lives determines where they shall spend eternity. More importantly, according to Ellen White, "A character formed according to the divine likeness is the only treasure that we can take from this world to the next" (*Christ's Object Lessons*, p. 142).

Now let's have a look at our more fleshed-out ladder, putting the three variables—imputed and imparted righteousness, relationship with God, and character development—together.

Figure 2: The Christian Ladder

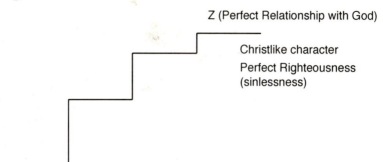

A—Imputed Righteousness (sinful but not wilful disobedience)
Deformnities of character still exist, and the relationship with God is cordial

The movement from A to Z depicts the path of the Christian experience. As people move from A to Z as noted above, three things will be happening simultaneously. First, their relationship with God grows and becomes intimate and personal until it is perfect; second, their characters change and develop until they become Christlike. Thirdly, they become perfect and righteous before God until they are sinless and holy. Therefore

    a. A person's character is the mirror image of his or her relationship with God. The development of a perfect and lasting relationship with God corresponds with the development of one's character.
    b. A person's perfection and righteousness (both imputed and imparted) and his or her relationship with God are two sides of the same coin. They vary positively.
    c. The development of Christlike character and perfection are also two sides of the same coin. The two also vary positively.

God calls His people to righteousness (perfection), Christlike character, and to a lasting relationship with Him. These three happen simultaneously in the Christian, yet the only tangible element of all these three dimensions from the human perspective is the development of character. Both perfection and a change in one's relationship with God are manifested in the character. As a result, a discussion about people's lasting relationship with God is a mirror image of a discussion about character development.

When people become Christians, they should begin to grow in their relationship with God, and, as noted above, this is evident through character development. The Lord requires growth from every Christian. As in nature there cannot be life without growth. Living things grow, or they die. Character development is not optional; it is imperative, necessary, and critical.

God plays a pivotal role in character development. According to the apostle Paul, it is God who begins the good work, who will carry it on, and who will complete it (see Phil. 1:3–8). It is God first and God last. "God has made provision that we may become like unto Him, and He will accomplish this for all who do not interpose a perverse will and thus frustrate His grace" (*Thoughts From the Mount of Blessing*, p. 76). God makes Christians blameless, pure, without fault (see Phil. 2:15), and Christlike when they trust Him.

God does nothing for individuals without their cooperation. They also have a part to play in their character development by cultivating the soil of their hearts so that God can transform them into His likeness. A Christian has to lay his or her life open to God's Spirit. Ellen White penned: "A noble, all-round character is not inherited. It does not come to us by accident. A noble character is earned by individual effort through the merits and grace of Christ" (*Christ's Object Lessons*, p. 331). Hard work is indispensable and critical in this area.

People's characters develop only as they are continually and constantly connected with God. Humanity is to cooperate with God, employing every power according to individual God-given ability. No branch can grow until and unless it is attached to the vine (see John 15:4–7). Similarly, apart from Christ there is no Christian growth and character development.

The development of our relationship with God ought to be supported; otherwise, it will be choked by the needs and problems of the world. Farmers know all too well that the field has to be continuously prepared and the plants pruned in order to facilitate proper growth (see John 15:2). Likewise, our relationship with God needs pruning and support. The process of character development is facilitated by discipleship, service, war with evil, obedience, constant communication with God, and suffering, as discussed in detail in subsequent chapters.

Is your character according to the divine likeness? If Christ were to come today or if you were to die today, would you be ready for the kingdom of God?

Chapter Seven

Learning Under the Master

Stand before God in the attitude of a learner
—Ellen G. White

Jesus commanded his followers to take His yoke upon themselves and learn from Him (Matt. 11:29). When one has repented and is reconciled with God, he or she does not graduate as a Christian or become perfect. On the contrary, the individual enters the school of God as a disciple. The individual stands before God first and foremost in the attitude of a learner. Learning as a disciple is the first and highest duty of every Christian.

> ## A Disciple
> A disciple is simply a learner, a student, who undergoes training, generally under a master, teacher, or leader; discipleship is an apprenticeship in the school of God. The word *disciple* means *follower of a master* and *a person who follows the discipline taught by a teacher*. In Ellen G. White's book *Acts of the Apostles*, the word *disciple* refers to those who confess Jesus as Christ. Disciples strive to be like their masters.

Discipleship is a process the disciple undergoes with and under the master during a period of training. Discipleship can best be understood as a school in which the master teaches, trains, grooms, and guides the student, who ultimately aspires to become like his master in trade and skill. This continuous, defined, and positive relationship suggests a special kind of attachment between the teacher and the disciple. A close bond forms between the teacher and scholar, who must work together in order for the training to be fruitful. The disciple seeks to learn from and please the master as much as possible. The experience of Jesus and His twelve disciples during His life on earth provide the model for discipleship. The twelve disciples underwent discipleship with Jesus for three and a half years. They had the unique opportunity of being trained under the greatest teacher ever known.

The commitment between master and student is such an integral part of the Christian experience that the Bible consistently refers to Christ's followers as "disciples." Discipleship plays a very critical role in the Christian's character development and maintenance of a lasting and positive relationship with God. The term *disciple* is synonymous with *Christian*. Christianity is discipleship. The more we learn as disciples of God, the more successful we, as Christians, become in developing our relationship with God.

Discipleship implies a continuous work toward maturity, the process of growing into new stages of knowledge and into a saving relationship with Jesus. When we are reconciled with God, we join a new kingdom totally alien to our old one; a new ruler with new rules, expectations, and requirements leads our lives. It is difficult, if not impossible, to have a lasting relationship with a person, let alone with God, if one does not know much about that person. Christians cannot grow in their relationship with God without a progressive knowledge of Him. The reconciled people have to learn more of their new master and their new kingdom with its requirements and norms. Discipleship therefore facilitates and catalyzes the development of a cordial relationship with God based on knowledge and not presumption. It contributes toward the development of the master's character in the disciple. The supreme object of discipleship is to groom disciples to be like their master.

By continuous revelation Christ endeavors to teach His people how to live, how to love Him as they develop an intimate relationship with Him. The Christian's learning process is endless. Jesus' disciples continued to learn even after they became apostles. The saints (believers) will definitely continue to learn in heaven. The Christian learning process only gets richer and more glorious with time; the more we learn of God, the more we will admire His character.

The design, content, method of instruction, and duration of the learning process is the prerogative of the master, who fully well discerns the individual disciple's requirements and situation.

How people learn depends on their individual willingness to do so. Some students learn fast and some slowly; some are serious and some not. God will not give people

Learning Under the Master

knowledge and wisdom if they neglect to see their need and are satisfied and content without it. This self-sufficiency causes Christian growth to become stagnant. Many Christians do not develop as fast in their relationship with God because they are not keen disciples.

The disciples of Jesus walked and talked with Him daily and witnessed all His dealings with the human race. They and their master essentially lived life together; they ate, prayed, rejoiced, and met troubles together. Ellen White elaborates: "On His journeys through country and cities, He took them with Him .... They travelled with Him from place to place. They shared the frugal fare, and like Him were sometimes hungry and often weary. On the crowded streets, by the lakeside, in the lonely desert, they were with Him" (*Acts of the Apostles*, p. 17). Similarly, we as Christ's disciples today are supposed to walk with, talk with, and learn from Him all the time.

Disciples do not work independently but work in collaboration with their master. As such, all disciples of Christ need constant guidance and support from the Master, without whom they cannot do anything.

The Master cares for and loves His disciples. Jesus always had the welfare of His disciples on His heart. He constantly prayed for them, individually and collectively, and He liked their company. He was patient with their misunderstanding and waywardness. Christians today are assured of the same kind of love, attention, care, and patience from their Master, Jesus.

Good as Well as Bad Disciples

Experience has shown that not all who enter the school of Christ achieve the desired result. Two classes of disciples emerge after undergoing the training: those who pass and those who fail. The same two classes of disciples emerged from Jesus' circle while He lived on earth. The training did not produce the desired result in the case of Judas, who betrayed his Master. The other 11 disciples graduated to become apostles after satisfactorily completing their discipleship. They strove to put into practice all of the Master's teachings, and this effort engendered development in their relationship with Him. Christians, as learners too, can either be good or bad disciples. Those disciples who fail to make the grade fail, in the process, to develop a positive and lasting relationship with God.

How Does One Learn as a Disciple of Christ?

There are several ways one may learn, including through Christian suffering and meditating upon the character of Christ (as articulated in subsequent chapters), but here we focus on reading and studying the Word of God. Through the study of God's Word, Christians grasp divine light, which is necessary to catalyze the development of noble and all-round characters in them.

God gave us His Word in order to instruct us (see Rom. 15:4). The Word of God, the Scriptures, the Bible, is the message of the Maker to humankind, the story of the Saviour and His love; above all, His words are the words of eternal life to His no longer immortal creation. God's Word is the expression of His thoughts.

God did not give us the Scriptures because He wanted

to be a famous author; He gave us the Scriptures because they contain life. Jesus reveals that His words are the foundation of a successful experience with God (see Matthew 7:24–27); therefore, all who are serious about their relationship with God will consistently and earnestly study the Bible, consulting its pages regularly; they will read it as they would a love letter *and* a lesson book. When people read God's Word, they learn how they may reach Him and cultivate a lasting relationship with Him. The Bible teaches us how to live in a cordial relationship with God. It even tells us what to avoid and what to do if we are in the wrong position and doing the wrong thing. It gives us straightforward, solid information about God's plans.

The Word of God is a rich treasure of wisdom and inspiration. Through its study Christians assimilate divine ideas, principles, and affections. It will mold their characters and lives after the divine likeness. If a Christian chooses to spend time studying God's Scriptures, the Author of that Word will become the Author of a well-balanced and noble character in that person's experience. People who earnestly and internally receive God's Word cannot remain unchanged. It is axiomatic that as people study the Word of God, they succeed in developing their relationship with God.

If you decide to believe, accept and submit to what God says in Scripture. He will give you the strength and energy to carry out the decision. Merely knowing what God says is not enough; it is important to put that knowledge into practice. Christians are to live according to every word of God (see Matt. 4:4) and obey God's Word conscientiously as they would an army order. Practice what it says in order to be holy.

Do you ever take time to really dig through the rich treasure of wisdom and inspiration in your quest to develop your relationship with God? Do you study the Bible like a lesson book? When confronted with the Word of God, what is your reaction? Do you receive it as true? Do you believe it? Do you submit to God's Word and put into practice what God says? Do you allow it to be a springboard for developing your relationship with God?

Chapter Eight

Working for the Master

We are to be God's helping hands in saving souls—channels through which His love is day by day to flow to the perishing—Ellen G. White

God ordained service as a divine agent through which Christians build their characters and develop their relationship with Him. Christians become Christlike as they work for God. In addition to bringing others to the Saviour, Christian service also has a far-reaching positive impact on the lives of those who embark on it. Though God could save sinners without the assistance of mortal and sinful beings, He chose to involve you and me for our own benefit. It is God's plan that men and women develop their relationship with Christ as they labour for Christ in serving humanity.

Reconciliation with God ushers the reconciled individual into service. The existence of a lasting relationship with God places the concerned Christian under obligation to serve his Master and his or her fellows. Christian service is not optional for true Christians. God allocates an individual, unique, and important work to each person. Every Christian should be involved in serving the Master in one way or another. Each person, whether young or old, educated or not, rich or poor, has work to do for the Master.

Serving has three major objectives that translate into benefits, namely the Christian will
1. develop a Christlike character,
2. enter into the Master's joy, and
3. bring others to Christ.

These are briefly elaborated below.

To Develop a Christlike Character

An important objective of Christian service is to develop noble, distinguished characters that engender a cordial relationship with God. People can develop Christlike characters only as they share in His work. As we labour in God's vineyard and cooperate with God in the work of saving souls, our characters are transformed into His likeness and our relationship with God is developed. As the Lord uses us to do His work, we shall not remain the same with respect to our relationship with God.

Service is God's ordained way for Christian growth. According to Ellen White, we understand God's word better as we share and explain it to others. We get more strength by doing something for Christ through service. Just as our bodies need exercise, we need to work for God to grow as Christians and to develop a christ-like character.

In addition, Christians acquire strength to resist evil through service. Through service Christians learn to put others before themselves.

Serving Secures Our Joy

Christ ordained service as a means for Christians to secure their joy. The joy of Christ is in seeing souls redeemed by His sacrifice, and Christians enter into that joy as they labour for the salvation of other people. Seeing lives transformed and changed brings a lot of joy to those serving. There is great truth in the hymn by Oswald Chambers: "There is joy in serving Jesus." Serving secures the Christian's joy in the Lord. Albert Schweitzer (1875 - 1965), the well known physician and philanthropist who served in Gabon, Africa; once told a group of students: "I do not know which will be the destiny of each of you; but one thing I know- the only ones among you who will be really happy will be those who have sought and found the way to serve."

Bringing Others to a Saving Relationship With Christ

All Christians are born into the kingdom of God as missionaries specifically ordained, qualified and equipped to work for the salvation of others. Their first desire and impulse as Christians is to also bring others to the Saviour. They become coworkers with Christ. To bring others to God, Christ does not choose unfallen angels but fallen human beings. Humanity is the channel to communicate with humankind. Indeed, God will not bring sinners to repentance without human agencies. Through faithful service God expects His people to help fellow humanity in sin to be reconciled with God.

Given the far-reaching effects service, or lack thereof, has, God holds all who do not participate in service guilty. All men and women are guilty before God if they do not make every effort possible to spread the good tidings of the grace of God to others.

Notwithstanding the many benefits of service, however, many Christians do very little for Christ. They do nothing to help fellow human beings or to further the kingdom of God. Herein lies the cause of stunted growth: Christians who do not serve do not grow in their relationship with God.

Christians serve when they do something good or work for others and God. There are several ways Christians can serve God in line with their distinct abilities. The work to be done entails giving to the world the good tidings of the grace of God. Christians can serve God by participating in evangelism, witnessing, nurturing young Christians, carrying other people's burdens, and visiting and distributing literature, as briefly discussed below:

Evangelism

Evangelism is one way Christians can serve God and humanity. Evangelism involves proclaiming the good news of Jesus Christ to the world, or presenting Bible teachings. It also involves presenting Jesus, who He is, what He has done, and what He has taught. Men and woman have been entrusted with the sacred mission of making known the riches of Christ. All of God's children should make this work top priority. Jesus says: "Go and make disciples of all nations, baptizing them in the name of the Father and of the Son and of the Holy Spirit, and teaching them to obey everything I have commanded you" (Matt. 28:19, 20). Those who receive the truth that the world needs are obliged to make it their first work to proclaim that same truth. The love of Christ can never be bottled up to be selfishly enjoyed by the possessor. Whenever an individual receives it, it will flow out to others. Everyone who is connected with God will impart light to others. If Christ dwells in the heart, the light will radiate to those around.

Witnessing

Although not all people can be evangelists or go as missionaries to foreign lands, all Christians can be Christ's witnesses. Witnessing is the art of wisely and lovingly leading others to discover an eternal relationship with Christ. Witnessing includes sharing and listening to our neighbors when they have a problem, giving a testimony to an unbeliever, or sharing the gospel through a Bible study. Christian witnessing is not a plan humans devised; God Himself ordained it. The Christian experience cannot be complete without it. Unbelievers need someone to witness to them because only by learning about Jesus and accepting His sacrifice can they be led to reconciliation with God.

Every Christian has got something to witness about. According to Ellen White:

> As witnesses for Christ, we are to tell what we know, what we ourselves have seen and heard and felt. If we have been following Jesus step by step, we shall have something right to the point to tell concerning the way in which He has led us. We can tell how we have tested His promise, and found the promise true. We can bear witness to what we have known of the grace of Christ. This is the witness for which our Lord calls, and for want of which the world is perishing. (*The Desire of Ages*, p. 340)

We do not need to be priests or pastors to be witnesses for Christ; if two demoniacs could witness for Christ, everyone can be a faithful witness. The two demoniacs had not been trained to preach nor had they attended seminary. However, they told others what they had seen and what they had experienced of God's favor in their own lives. Each person who has had an encounter with Christ has something to tell the world about God's power.

Christ told the man from whom He had cast out demons the following: "Return home and tell how much God has done for you" (Luke 8:39). Similarly, Christ expects all Christians to go tell the world what God has done for them.

Nurturing Young Christians

Many Christian workers concentrate on bringing people to Christ and the church, but do little to help them grow. The converted need to be looked after; they need to be nursed—in the form of watchful attention, help, and encouragement. Satan and his agents pursue those who come to Christ, seeking to gather them back to his ranks. As a result, many new members become discouraged, linger by the way, and are left at the mercy of devouring wolves. They come in through the front door but quickly leave through the back door.

God grants His church the responsibility to nurse those who are young in faith and experience. This involves a wide array of activities, including praying with them and helping and encouraging them. It may also involve offering sympathy and instruction and helping them carry their burdens (see Gal. 6:2). All Christians, especially new Christians, need help and encouragement from fellow Christians from time to time. All Christians are admonished to be an encouragement to others.

Visitation and Distribution of Literature

All Christians can play a role in distributing publications. The gospel in the form of the written word, in published works, needs to be carried to all people. In some cases, the written word is the only way the gospel can reach some people.

Training for Service

All Christians need training in order to be effective in God's service. There are many Christians who are willing to work for God if only they knew how to begin; they need to be instructed and encouraged. Thus, every church should operate as a training school for Christian workers, with the supreme object of teaching Christian workers to work for God and to depend on Him. Ellen White recommends that in the school, "members should be taught how to give Bible readings [or Bible studies], how to teach, how best to care for the poor and to care for the sick, how to work for the unconverted" (*The Ministry of Healing*, p. 149).

Are you willing to cooperate with Jesus in judiciously laboring for others, however humble and unappreciated the work may seem? Are you willing and able to fully surrender self for the cause of service? Are you willing to use every physical, moral, and mental power in laboring together with God? Are you willing to sacrifice the conveniences of time, home, town, family, church, country, and even life itself to reach the people who have not been reached by the gospel? Will you devote yourself actively and unreservedly to God's service?

Chapter Nine

War With the Devil

Be sober, be vigilant; because your adversary the devil, as a roaring lion, walketh about, seeking whom he may devour—1 Peter 5:8, KJV

All who have been reconciled with God and are developing their relationship with Him soon discover that they have to contend with an opposing force that will attack and assail them day and night. The reality of the evil one rarely becomes more glaring in one's life than when one is reconciled with God. God's enemy, the devil, is and has been at war against all those who side with God by developing a relationship with Him (see Rev. 12:17).

As we have discussed, reconciliation with God is a gesture that unequivocally defines our relationship with God, rendering God as Friend and Father. However, it also defines, just as starkly, our "relationship" with the devil—namely, declaring him our enemy. A decision to follow Christ thus is an open declaration of war with the evil one. The devil is enraged and his enmity aroused and kindled when people who have been under his control now decidedly choose to get along well with God. When one subject of Satan's kingdom repents, Satan is aroused to resist. The war with the devil is triggered by and is a certain result of entering and maintaining a lasting relationship with God.

James asked: "Do you not know that friendship with the world is enmity with God? Therefore whoever wishes to be a friend of the world makes himself the enemy of God" (James 4:4), and the reverse is also true. When people live in sin they are said to be "children of wrath" and to be under the dominion of Satan (e.g., Eph. 2:3). They do his biddings (knowingly or not) and serve him as their master.

Individuals who decide to have a relationship with God take a stand in the battle against Satan. It is not possible to be cordially related with God and yet at the same time not meet hostility and hatred from the devil. Being hated by the devil is not optional but comes with the package—a part and parcel of being a Christian. All true Christians will, no doubt, have to fight the wiles of the devil. Even Christ had a torrid time and battle with the evil one throughout his life. Every human heart or mind is the battle ground for the spiritual warfare between Satan and God.

The enmity between Satan and Christians does not only occur at the beginning of the journey but continues right through the process of developing a relationship with God. As a result, developing and maintaining a relationship with God will not always be easy and trouble-free and will be littered with difficulties and opposition throughout. Christians need not deceive themselves in thinking that they will not have opposition, problems, and difficulties in their experiences. Some inexplicable trials and situations will arise, and Christians will be treated unjustly and will suffer reproach or persecution for their faith because of the devil's work. There is no end to one's struggle with self and sin in this life. The existence and reality of the war with the evil one in your life should not worry you but should give you the assurance that you are indeed reconciled with God. It is only worrisome when the devil does not consider your life enough of a threat to have to bother you.

The war between Satan and God is no pastime. It is not there for a thrill, fascination, or adventure to entice participants in a game of daring and winning. It is a serious means to a serious spiritual end. The devil wishes to achieve a defined spiritual result, and he puts forth all his superhuman effort to accomplish this through spiritual warfare. The devil's objective is to tempt people to doubt and to deny God and thereby spoil or discontinue their relationship with Him. Satan is always working to deceive, accuse, intimidate, and misrepresent the people of God. He has tailor-made devices for every soul.

The War Is Spiritual

The war between Satan and Christians is spiritual. Paul wrote, "For our struggle is not against flesh and blood, but against the rulers, against the authorities, and against the powers of this dark world and against the spiritual forces of evil in the heavenly realms" (Eph. 6:12). Paul also wrote: "The weapons we fight with are not the weapons of the world. On the contrary, they have divine power to demolish strongholds" (2 Cor. 10:4). In secular wars soldiers put on an amor; similarly, there is an amor for Christians (see Eph. 6:13).

As a result of the devil's persistent and determined efforts, some Christians who enter into a relationship with God may fail to finish the race. Many of those who are involved in the war with the devil will be tempted to think that God has forsaken them, and stumble or fall on the way. Some will fail to persevere in the Lord.

> ### The War Was Won by Christ
> The Bible says that the war between God and Satan is no longer a contest but a decided case. Christ, by His mission and death, gained the victory over Satan. The devil is a defeated foe. What is now left to be decided is who will side with God and who will side with Satan, through the exercise of freewill choice. Christ's victory enables everyone to conquer the devil. You do not need to invent victory; you only need to side with Christ, and His victory becomes yours. Christians are assured of God's enduring presence in all their battles and, most importantly, their victory.

Realizing the devil's seriousness and determination, the apostle Peter wrote: "Be self-controlled and alert. Your enemy the devil prowls around like a roaring lion, looking for someone to devour" (1 Pet. 5:8). If the devil is like a lion, it takes all time-alertness, watchfulness, and vigilance to resist his attacks. Christians need not take chances but "be instant in season, out of season" (2 Tim. 4:2, KJV). They cannot afford to relax, or seek repose or rest, lest they get caught unawares. Indeed, there is no resting place for a Christian on this earth.

Christians need the whole armor of God, most importantly, in order to be able to stand against the devil's schemes in the war. Having part of the armor is not good enough; you must have it in totality. The Christian armor includes the breastplate of righteousness, the shield of faith, the helmet of salvation, the sword of the spirit—the Word of God, and alertness, among others (Eph. 6:13–17).

Chapter Ten

Christian Loyalty

Now by this we may know that we know him, if we keep His Commandments—1 John 2:4, NKJV

People are by nature "children of disobedience" (Eph. 2:2, KJV) and naturally do what pleases them rather than what pleases God. When people are reconciled with God and are developing a relationship with God, it will manifest in a new desire to be loyal to God and to do His bidding. True faith will invariably manifest in obedience. Loyalty to God is as vitally united to right relationship with God as breathing to life, or body to soul. It is impossible for a heart that is subdued by the love of God to be devoid of loyalty to God. The Bible says, "The man who says, 'I know him,' but does not do what he commands is a liar, and the truth is not in him" (1 John 2:4).

It is through obedience that a Christian cultivates a relationship with God and achieves character development. Loyalty and obedience to God is the mechanism and process by which we form a Christlike character and relinquish our sinful and carnal nature. Ellen White wrote: "As in obedience to His natural laws the earth should produce its treasures, so in obedience to His moral law the hearts of the people were to reflect the attributes of His character" (*Christ's Object Lessons*, p. 124).

Obedience, therefore, lies at the core of true Christian living. Paul wrote: "You are slaves to the one whom you obey—whether you are slaves to sin, which leads to death, or to obedience, which leads to righteousness" (Rom. 6:16). Christians become servants of Christ and begin to obey him the moment they become free from the bondage of sin.

In the natural world, all things obey God's law. Through the laws of nature, all of God's creation, except sinful people, yield implicit and perfect obedience to His command. It is only in obedience to these laws that all things in nature grow and develop. Similarly, it is only by observing the laws of harmony that a musician can compose good music. It is only by observing the rules of the game that an athlete can play and win. Humankind must obey God's law in order to be in harmony with Him. The Lord expects from each soul, from Adam to the last person, perfect obedience and unblemished righteousness. True Christians will inquire at every step of the walk with God, "is this the way of the Lord?"

Loyalty and God's Law

God's holy law defines and is the expression of God's character and His will. In order for one to live in harmony with God, he or she must live according to the principles and directions of God's law. The law of God stands for everyone as a test of obedience, faith, and love to God. Obedience and disobedience are invariably linked to adherence and non-adherence to the law of God.

God gave His people, from ancient Israel to the present generation, the law—the everlasting principles of truth, justice and purity, for their benefit. Lutzer Elwin in the book *When a Good Man Falls* noted that although sheep, aside from the default virtue of being sheep, don't have to do anything to be accepted by the shepherd, their individual levels of obedience directly affect their welfare: the more obedient they are to the shepherd, the better it is for them because he watches and cares for them. A shepherd is responsible for his sheep. Similarly, the more obedient people are to God the better for them. Obedience to the law of God is to our advantage (individually and collectively). Through obedience we assimilate God's character, prove our love for Him, and save ourselves from our own self-destructive, sinful practices.

Loyalty and Love

As spiritual children of God, Christians ought to obey their Father in heaven as earthly children their fathers on earth. Children obey their fathers not to buy their love or some favours but because of love for them. Similarly as children of God, we obey Him because we love Him and because He loved us first. All God's children demonstrate and prove their love for God through obedience (see 1 John 5:3). Genuine obedience from the heart is motivated by love. Jesus summed up God's law in Matthew 22:37–39: "'Love the Lord your God will all your heart and with all your soul and with your entire mind.' This is the first and greatest commandment. And the second is like it. 'Love your neighbor as yourself.'" Love for God and fellow individuals is inseparable from loyalty to God.

Christians are elevated, ennobled, and blessed through obedience. Those who refuse to abide by the divine principles as expressed in the holy law place themselves outside the channel where God's blessings flow. Many of God's blessings are conditional on obedience to God's law or commandments (see Deut. 7:11–15). More so, obedience is the condition of eternal life—the same condition that was required of Adam and Eve before their fall. Christ said, "If you want to enter life, obey the commandments" (Matt. 19:17). Before we can be rendered eternally secure, our loyalty (obedience) to God must prove our right relationship with God. Obedience, perfect and perpetual, is the condition of eternal happiness.

Which Law?

To Jesus' answer, "Obey the commandments," the rich young ruler, like many Christians today, responded, "Which ones?" Christ referred the rich young man to the divine precepts, the immutable law that has been there since the foundation of the earth. He referred him to the moral law as given in the Ten Commandments (Matt. 19:16–19; see Exod. 20).

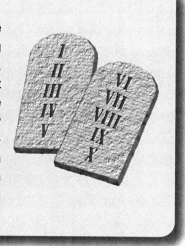

Loyalty to God is the criteria for distinguishing those who have a lasting relationship with God and those who do not. Obedience is a sign of a transformed life. "Here is the true test. If we abide in Christ, if the love of God dwells in us, our feelings, our thoughts, our purposes, our actions, will be in harmony with the will of God," wrote Ellen White (*Steps to Christ*, p. 51).

The right relationship between God and human beings is soured through disobedience. Disloyalty to God is a sure sign of the existence of a soured and fractured relationship between people and God.

There are many, however, who claim that the law was abrogated by the death of Christ and that Christians no longer need to observe the law. Preempting such claims, Christ said: "Think not that I am come to destroy the law, or the prophets.... Till heaven and earth pass, one jot or one title shall in no wise pass from the law" (Matt. 5:17, 18, KJV). The death of Jesus Christ on the cross did not destroy or abrogate the law. Christ did not lessen the claims of the law by His life and death. On the contrary, Jesus' death proved that the law cannot be changed. If the law could be changed, it would not have been necessary for Christ to die. God's law is indeed immutable.

Jesus lived a life of perfect obedience to the Father and thus left us an example to follow. He was obedient to the point of submitting to die on the cross. Jesus, by His perfect obedience to God, proved that with divine help sinful human beings can obey all of God's laws. In addition, Christ gives us the power to obey God's law.

Obedience to God's law is a pleasure for every regenerated soul. If a Christian wants to enjoy life, he or she must learn to live in harmony with the law of God (see James 1:25, 2:12). Without the law there can only be chaos and frustration.

As the earth's history moves toward its climax, there will be only two classes of people on earth: those who keep the commandments of God and the faith of Jesus, and those who disobey Him. Every person's character will show whether one has chosen the side of loyalty or that of rebellion. Which side will you be on? Won't you decide to enter into the joy of obedience given the many promises and blessings it will bring in your life?

Chapter Eleven

Christian Suffering

The trials of life are God's workman, to remove the impurities and toughness from our character
—Ellen G. White

God permits all Christians who are developing their relationship with Him to encounter trials, persecution, and hardships for their benefit. Nobody who is in a cordial relationship with God is exempt from trials and suffering; on the contrary, these hardships come as part of the package. In developing their characters, all Christians at various points in their lives inevitably go down the pathway of suffering.

Suffering Types

People suffer in many different ways. Some suffer from poverty, wars, sickness, stress, death of loved ones, while others suffer from marital, family, and vocational challenges. Still others, like Paul, suffer from persecution, abuse, hunger, thirst, and more, all for the sake of Christ.

Afflictions test the characters of God's people. Persecution and suffering are instrumental in testing the character and the genuineness of people's relationship with God. Such trials quell fierce passions. They reveal the state of the heart—weaknesses, faults, blemishes, and perils.

Christian Suffering

Suffering refines and polishes Christian characters. One songwriter wrote:

> The trials of life are God's workman, to remove the impurities and toughness from our character. Their hewing, squaring, and chiselling, their burning and polishing, is a painful process; it is hard to be pressed down to the grinding wheel. But the stone is brought forth prepared to fill its place in the heavenly temple.[9]

According to Ellen White, "the Lord permits trials that we may be cleansed from earthliness, from selfishness, from harsh, un-Christlike traits of character. He suffers the deep waters of affliction to cover our souls in order that we may have deep heart longings to be cleansed from defilement and may come forth from trial purer, holier and happier" (*Christ's Object Lessons*, p. 71). Paul wrote: "Not only so, but we also rejoice in our sufferings, because we know that suffering produces perseverance; perseverance, character; and character, hope" (Rom. 5:3, 4). Suffering burns out the dross of selfishness and worldliness. Job exclaimed, "He knoweth the way that I take: when he hath tried me, I shall come forth as gold" (Job 23:10, KJV).

Christian suffering was ordained by God for our training in building our characters. God teaches us obedience, patience, and submission by the things we suffer (see Heb. 5:8). We grow in our faith as we suffer with and for Christ.

The cruel blow that blights the joys of earth is a means of turning our eyes to heaven. There are many out there who would never have known God had not sorrow led them to seek comfort in Him. Persecution, sickness, the loss of sight, hearing or limb, the loss of property, or other calamities may likewise be instrumental in drawing us nearer to God (see Psalm 119:71; Isa. 26:9). Henry Ward Beecher observed that troubles are often the tools by which God fashions us for better things.

Suffering is bitter and not pleasant, but whatever the cause, it should help Christians mold and develop the right relationship with God. Through suffering Christians learn something they would probably not learn through any other way. More importantly, fellowship with Christ in suffering is the highest honor ever bestowed upon humankind.

The reality of suffering notwithstanding, Scriptures teach that God does not cause people to suffer. God does not willingly bring sorrows upon people or afflict them in order to grieve them (see Lam. 3:31–33).

All people suffer for four main reasons, including commonplace circumstances, our own sin and foolishness, our need for discipline, and attacks from the devil. These are discussed briefly below:

The Common Lot of Humanity

In the beginning, as we have observed in Chapter 1, the first human beings did not experience suffering, pain, or sorrow before they sinned. Their fall opened floodgates for woe and suffering in the world. As a result, Christians and non-Christians alike suffer because they are part of a fallen humanity and live in a fallen world. God allows people to suffer and experience pain because He gave them real choices with real consequences. The earth is under a curse because of sin (see Gen. 3: 17). All humanity, including Christians, suffers from war, sickness, fractured friendships, degenerative diseases, and death. Just as the sun shines on the just and unjust, so bacteria invade the bodies of both sinner and saint. Clearly, a sinful world cannot be free of suffering.

Our Own Fault (Sins, Stupidity, Foolishness)

Through poor choices, people invite suffering upon their own lives and families and on the lives of others. In much of human suffering, the connection between sin and suffering is direct and obvious. Many people in the world, for example, are sick and in some cases die of cancer on account of cigarette smoking. Alcoholism, sexual perversion, and gambling, to name only a few of the widespread self-destructive addictions, have caused (and continue to cause) suffering on so many levels. Such practices bring untold suffering not only on the person who intentionally involve themselves but also to their families and to society in general. Through poor choices, both Christians and non-Christians invite suffering.

Surely, there is a connection between sin and suffering. However, certainly not every sin receives its appropriate penalty or consequence in this life. In other words, sometimes consequences are not direct and immediate but become evident much later. And sometimes the consequences *are* immediate but instead affect the innocent bystander, so to speak, rather than the primary sinner. Often a person's foolishness will first adversely affect someone else. It is important to note, then, that suffering is not necessarily an index of the sufferer's sinfulness; we live in a sin-sick world and nobody can remain unaffected by the pain, sorrow, and suffering that have become ubiquitous after the fall. Thus, human selfishness and sin, collectively considered, explains much if not most of human woe.

Discipline

Christians also suffer by way of discipline. It is on record that God occasionally and where necessary disciplines those He loves by permitting suffering to befall them. God never originates evil or suffering, but certainly He does at times allow suffering to befall men and women to purify, teach, or test them. The Bible says, "For whom the Lord loveth he chasteneth, and scourgeth every son whom he receiveth" (Heb. 12:6, KJV).

Attacks From the Evil One

Christians, by deciding to follow Christ, additionally face a unique kind of suffering. This type of suffering is challenging and complex. People may suffer and experience misery even when they have done nothing wrong or

Christian Suffering

when it isn't their own fault. The devil champions this suffering. Christians suffer indiscriminately from the attacks and violence orchestrated by Satan. He brings problems into the lives of Christians to make them question and doubt the presence of God and His leading in their lives. The devil uses suffering as a tool to achieve his own intended aim of spoiling the cordial relationship between a person and God. This is what Paul referred to in his letter to Timothy when he wrote that all people who will live a godly life would suffer (see 2 Tim. 3:12).

The life and mission of the apostle Paul is a practical example of suffering that the devil instigates. It seems that the more Paul served God the more he suffered. Wherever he went, things did not go smoothly. He suffered all kinds of abuses; being jailed, beaten, mocked, interrogated, and shipwrecked were only several of the multiple hardships Paul faced during his missions. All these difficulties occurred because of the devil's work. Nearly all dedicated Christians experienced this suffering, including Stephen, one of the seven deacons; James and John, the sons of Zebedee; Peter, and many others. Some were stoned to death, others jailed, crucified, beaten, and tortured for their faith. In subsequent eras, such as during the Dark Ages, for example, Christians continued to undergo persecution; Martin Luther is only one of countless examples. Christ also experienced this kind of suffering. The prophet Isaiah referred to Christ as the suffering servant (Isa. 52:13–15). He left heaven and all its glories to suffer and die for the human race. Suffering was no easier for Jesus to face than it is for us.

The last two suffering types above (God's discipline or the devil's attacks) are unique to the Christian experience. The subsequent discussion in this chapter focuses on these types of suffering and their role in shaping, developing, and molding the Christian's relationship with God.

> ## Suffering Can Disturb the Christian's Relationship With God
>
> Suffering, if not endured with perseverance, may disturb the Christian's cordial relationship with God. The Scriptures contain numerous examples of men and women who under suffering denied that they ever knew God or had a relationship with Him. John Mark, for example, due to the perils and ordeals he suffered wavered from serving God for a time. "Unused to hardships, he [Mark] was disheartened by the perils and privations of the way. He had laboured with success under favorable circumstances, but now, amidst the opposition and perils that so often beset the pioneer worker, he failed to endure hardness as a good soldier of the cross.... As the apostles advanced, and still greater difficulties were apprehended, Mark was intimidated and, losing all courage, refused to go further and returned to Jerusalem." (*Acts of the Apostles*, pp. 169, 170).

God is aware of all the suffering that takes place on the earth. In fact, nothing befalls a person that God did not permit. Though God is almighty and omnipotent to the extent that He can effectively command all Christian suffering in the world to cease. Instead, in numerous instances, He states that suffering is inevitable to those who come to Him. Those who suffer for Christ are called blessed (see Matt. 5:10–12; Acts 5:40–42). Many of those who will be in heaven will have passed through great trials and suffering on this earth (see Rev. 7:14).

While God does not instruct Christians to avoid suffering, He is faithful to give them sufficient strength and wisdom for each situation and emergency. God only allows that which His providence sees best to befall His people. Much more importantly, He helps His people go safely through whatever may befall them and watches over them. According to Ellen White, "the eyes of the Savior are above us, around us, noting every difficulty, discerning every danger; and there is no place where his eyes cannot penetrate, no sorrows and sufferings of his people where the sympathy of Christ does not reach" (*That I May Know Him*, p. 360). Paul wrote that God is faithful and "will not let you be tempted beyond what you can bear. But when you are tempted, he will also provide a way out so that you can stand up under it" (1 Cor. 10:13). God does not leave you alone when you are suffering. Whatever your sorrow or loneliness, you have a sympathizing friend.

When God's children suffer, God suffers with them. Your afflictions, pain, discomfort, and woes are not confined to you alone. Whatever you undergo, God feels it with you. Do you suffer from disease, rejection, loneliness, and anxiety? Do you lack anything? Remember, God feels and suffers with you.

How Should God's People Best Meet Suffering?

Whether suffering will have a negative or positive effect on the Christian's life and relationship with God depends much on how he or she responds to it. If properly received, the trial that seems so bitter and hard to bear will prove to be a blessing. Christians should give thanks in all circumstances (1 Thess 5:18) including in the midst of their suffering, not *for* the suffering but *in* it. They give thanks to God because His grace is sufficient and because He is well able to deliver them and will do so in His own time.

Peter urges Christians not to consider suffering and trial as if it were something strange. He wrote "Dear friends, do not be surprised at the painful trial you are suffering, as though something strange were happening to you. But rejoice that you participate in the sufferings of Christ" (1 Pet. 4:12, 13). According to the apostle Peter, by sharing in Jesus' suffering we will also share in His glory. All things, including suffering, work together for good to those who love God (Rom. 8:28).

Citizens of Heaven

The critical and pertinent ingredient to maintaining a lasting relationship with God irrespective of all the negative situations we may experience is to focus on heaven. The more one cherishes heaven and fastens the mind upon the future life and its blessedness, in comparison with the temporal concerns of this world, the easier it will be to live the way God expects of him or her. None of the mishaps and negative situations will be a hindrance to Christians if they fasten their minds on the future glory.

Christian Suffering

Is your character indomitable to the point that adverse circumstances cannot overthrow you? Do you have a strong moral backbone that cannot be terrified even by suffering? Such will be the character of all who are truly developing a relationship with God.

---

9   Author unknown

Chapter Twelve

Talking With God

Then He spoke a parable to them, that men always ought to pray and not lose heart—Luke 18:1, NKJV.

Effective communication is essential to the establishment, maintenance, and development of solid human relationships. As in human relationships, communication plays an integral role in establishing and maintaining a Christian's relationship with God. The communication between a Christian and God occurs through prayer. To develop and maintain a lasting relationship with God, Christians need to talk to Him through prayer.

God, like earthly parents, values listening and talking to His children because they are precious to Him and He loves them very much (see Isa. 43:4). He does not forsake His children, and He does not let His children down. He is more willing to give good things to those who ask Him than an earthly father is (see Luke 11:11–13). God has only good thoughts toward each and every person (see Jer. 29:11). God is always near those who seek Him (see Deut. 4:7). He wants to shower blessings upon His children, but God desires that His children spend time with Him through prayer. He beckons Christians, no matter how humble, to talk to Him. God's ears are attentive to the prayers of His followers (1 Peter 3:13).

Why Pray?

Prayer is not intended to inform God of something He does not already know, because God is omniscient. God knows everything about everybody all the time (see 1 John 3:20; Ps. 44:21). God knows and sees everything—our thoughts, our heart's desires, our past, our present, and our future. People do not pray to convince God to have mercy of them, because He is merciful and always kind to them. So why should Christians pray?

Within the context of establishing and maintaining our relationship with God, prayer has many benefits. First, God moves and acts in response to our asking/praying. The Bible says, "ask, and it shall be given to you; seek, and ye shall find" (Matt. 7:7, KJV). There is an "if" and "then" relationship in this verse. We first ask and then God responds (e.g., gives) through answering our prayers (see 1 Chron. 5:20). God's actions in Christians' lives are dependent on their prayers. God genuinely wants to answer our prayers. One of the reasons why so little of God's power is manifested in the world is because people sporadically pray or do not pray at all. Through prayer, we ask and receive many other blessings such as God's presence, forgiveness for sins, and His guidance. From my personal experience, when God manifests His power in my life in response to my prayers, it gives me more confidence in Him. It moves me to a higher level in my Christian experience.

Second, prayer gives Christians energy and strength to fight the devil and to resist temptation. Through prayer, we access God's grace, which upholds us in times of trials and temptations. It is only when we are connected with God that we will be able to conquer the devil. Without prayer, we are at great risk of falling into sin.

Third, Christians are changed as they pray. When you are in constant connection with God through prayer, you cannot remain the same—your life is forever changed. By beholding God and His love, righteousness, and mercy, we are changed into His likeness. The more we spend time talking and interacting with God, the more we will become like Him and less like the world.

Fourth, Christians deepen their relationship with God as they pray. Prayer brings people closer to God. People who pray feel a closer and more intimate connection with God than those who do not. In raising our minds and hearts to God through prayer, we enter into His presence and thus place ourselves in line with God.

The bottom-line is that prayer is important for spiritual development and contributes toward the development of a renewed and intimate relationship between us and God. Prayer is more than asking God for something. It is an act of worship, adoration, and a way for us to spend time with God. Prayer is primarily for our sake, not God's.

Prayer—Matter of the Heart and Lifestyle

Communicating with God through prayer is more than just an exchange of facts and opinions; it is primarily a matter of the heart. At the core of prayer is the heart-to-heart communication between a Christian and

God. Through prayer all people can pour out their hearts to God. In prayer people share their sorrows, joys, fears, plans, insecurities, nakedness, vulnerabilities, and fears. Prayer can also occur without words. It is fine to go to God and just cry out to Him. He understands our deepest hurts and He longs to be near to us.

Heart-to-heart and personal prayer does not happen the moment we start our relationship with God or by accident. Like in human relationships, our prayers may start out dry, brief, or businesslike. Over time, however, as our relationship with God grows these prayers develop to become more personal and intimate. The closer and intimate the relationship becomes, the more personal and intimate our prayers will become. John Powell describes the following five levels of human communication in the book *"Why Am I Afraid to Tell You Who I Am"*: cliché, fact, opinion, emotion, and transparency. At the beginning of our relationship with God, our prayer life starts out simple (e.g., cliché) but it should develop until it is transparent—being completely open with God and talking to Him from our heart.

Prayer should not be an event or something we do once in a while, but it should be a lifestyle. This prayer lifestyle does not occur by accident or without effort given the many factors that work against us and distract us from achieving such a lifestyle. To achieve such a lifestyle, each person should make conscious choices and behavioral modifications to facilitate it. For example, we need to desire God's presence through prayer. In addition, we need to devote time toward this lifestyle.

We ought to pray in all occasions (see Luke 18:1; 1 Thess. 5:17)—anywhere, anytime, and under any circumstance (see Eph. 6:18). There is need for consistency and persistence in prayer. Do not quit or become weary of praying. Jesus said, "Men always ought to pray and not lose heart" (Luke 18:1, NKJV). When you honestly ask God for something you desire and continue to trust Him to give it to you, He is more likely to do it. God values and rewards persistent prayer. As with Jacob, wrestle with God in prayer as if your life depends on it, which it does.

Approaching God in Prayer

First, it is important to appreciate the important role of faith in prayer. The Bible says, "And without faith it is impossible to please God, because anyone who comes to him must believe that he exists and that he rewards those who earnestly seek him" (Heb. 11:6). Faith is belief and trust in God. Christians ought to believe that God exists and that He listens to them and cares for them. We may not intellectually understand the complete functioning of prayer, but in faith, we need to pray nonetheless, trusting in God's providence. In many other aspects of life, we do not understand how things fully work (e.g., airplanes), but we still use them.

Second, as sinners, people cannot commune with a righteous and perfect God without an intercessor or mediator. Jesus is the only mediator between believers and God. There is nothing that you and I can do or not do that will make our prayers acceptable to God. Our prayers are not heard and answered by God based on our own merits; they are based on the merits of what Jesus Christ did on the cross. Our prayers are accepted by God because of Christ's faithfulness alone. We do not have to be perfect to approach God in prayer. This should add a dose of humility to our prayers.

Third, because of association with sin, we cannot pray or talk in the language that God can understand and accept, especially at the beginning of our relationship with God. However, God provided a solution for this in that whenever we pray, God's spirit intercedes on our behalf. God's spirit takes our utterances—no matter how feeble they may be—and translates and packages them in a way that God can accept and answer them favorably. An understanding of this important role of God's Spirit is encouraging, liberating, and empowering. Therefore, we all ought to be real and authentic, saying what we mean before God. We do not have to struggle to find the right language or use perfect words because God's Spirit is available to help.

Fourth, God grants each person free and open access to Himself through prayer. You do not need a priest, minister, pastor, or someone else to approach God on your behalf, for God hears and accepts the prayers of His followers directly from them. All Christians have equal and open access to the throne of God. What a special privilege and a unique opportunity and honor this is.

Finally, those developing a relationship with God ought to approach the throne of grace with confidence and boldness. The Bible says, "Let us then approach the throne of grace with confidence, so that we may receive mercy and find grace to help us in our time of need" (Heb. 4:16). The Bible does not say some Christians have confidence and others do not—all Christians, individually and collectively, have confidence. In Ephesians 3:12, Paul also encourages Christians to approach God with freedom and confidence. We ought to be confident that God will pay attention to us. This confidence in approaching God is not based on what we have done or not done, or how "good" we think we are or not. There is no need for hesitancy, doubt, and uncertainty on your part as you approach God. Freely and boldly come to God's presence in prayer.

Through prayer, we reach out to God and communicate with Him. Our relationship with God cannot develop without a consistent and effective prayer life. Our relationship with God will be lasting, loving, personal, and intimate if we take time and effort to talk to God and to draw nearer to Him through prayer.

The more you pray, the more you will be acquainted with Him and will be transformed into His likeness. Set aside time in the morning, afternoon, evening, and night to speak to Him and spend time with Him. Prayer should be an ongoing and ever deepening process for all people who desire a relationship with God.

Chapter Thirteen

I Fall Yet I Rise Again

Our glory is not in never falling but in rising every time we fall—Ellen G. White

People who are developing a lasting relationship with God would have at some point asked (or will indeed ask at some point in the future): If I sin, does that mean that I have not been reconciled with God? What happens if I sin with respect to my relationship with God? Has my relationship with God been broken? Does reconciliation with God eliminate the struggle with sin? Do I have to start all over again?

To be reconciled and redeemed implies to cease to sin. When we are reconciled with God, we are expected not to sin. John wrote, "My dear children, I write this to you so that you will not sin" (1 John 2:1). Christians are called to sinless living. The reconciled people's quest is for perfection. John wrote, "No one who is born of God will continue to sin" (1 John 3:9). Does this mean that those who have been reconciled with Christ do not sin? Certainly not!

Those who follow Christ and are reconciled with God are not beyond falling. They remain fallible. No matter how sincere our conversion may be, none of us is sinless. No matter how strong our profession and dedication to Christ may be, none of us is beyond falling or sinning.

Falling into sin is possible for all people on this side of eternity. All people, the righteous and the non-righteous, fall into sin, have fallen into sin, or will fall into sin at one point. The Bible says, "all have sinned and fall short of the glory of God" (Rom. 3:23). All Christians struggle with sin and also fall into sin. John wrote, "But if anybody does sin..." thus acknowledging that even Christians are susceptible to sin (1 John 2:1). Jesus also recognized that His followers would not be perfect, or sinless.

The Scriptures include a record of righteous men and women who also fell into sin. In fact, heroes of faith such as Solomon, David, Abraham, Peter, Moses, and Job fell at some point in their lives, committing grave sins before God. Even those whom God greatly blessed and favored were not sinless. Though John the Baptist, David, Enoch, and Elijah, among others, were largely considered to be good examples of Christian living, they were not exempt from sinning.

Jedidiah Was Fallible Too!

Concerning the life and fall of Solomon, Ellen G. White noted: "He who had been honored of God with tokens of divine favor so remarkable that his wisdom and uprightness gained for him worldwide fame, he who had led others to ascribe honor to the God of Israel, turned from the worship of Jehovah to bow before the idols of the heathen" (*Prophets and Kings*, p. 20).

The Bible says: "As Solomon grew old, his wives turned his heart after other gods, and his heart was not fully devoted to the Lord his God, as the heart of David his father had been. He followed Ashtoreth the goddess of the Sidonians, and Molech the

(cont.)

> detestable god of the Ammonites. So Solomon did evil in the eyes of the Lord; he did not follow the Lord completely" (1 Kings 11:4–5). Solomon, though wise, powerful, and, above all, favored of God was fallible still. He, too, was overcome by temptation and fell into sin.

The lives and experiences of the many "good" people in the Bible indeed confirm that even the best of God's people were and are fallible. Great men and women who were entrusted with great responsibilities were sometimes overcome by temptation, and committed sins, even as we also waver and frequently fall into sin. They did not cease to be mortal, frail, and fallible. Similarly, people who have been called by God do not upon repentance immediately become perfect and sinless or affixed to doing right.

However, the Bible says, "Whoever is a child of God does not continue to sin, because God's very nature is in him" (1 John 3:9, TEV). John meant that no one who is a Christian makes sin the habitual practice of his or her life. Therefore, there is a difference in the sins committed by the reconciled people and the sinning done by those who have no relationship with or have no knowledge of God. The fundamental distinction is drawn between *habitual* sinning and *occasional* sinning. John says those born of God are not guilty of the former, though occasionally they do sin, sometimes unknowingly, unintentionally, or simply momentarily at points of weakness. A true believer cannot engage in wilful or known sin and remain a true believer.

Reconciliation guarantees that we will not habitually sin. It is not a good omen if a Christian continues committing habitual sin. Those having a relationship with God will hate or dislike what they know to be offensive to their Father.

In the same vein, the Bible says, "But if anybody does sin..." (1 John 2:1), and as Ty Gibson in *The Path of the Just* observes, John does not say "*when* we sin ..." which would have somewhat nonchalantly suggested that we should expect to sin; rather, it says "if," meaning *in case*. It is not a light matter. To John, and thus to God, sin is not a matter of *when* but rather *if* for the child of God.

It is also important to note that sinning in the case of the reconciled people is not the end but is always followed by the "rising up" again. Christians do not give up in despair if they sin but instead repent and receive pardon for all sins committed. It is that simple.

Sin and Christians' Relationship With God

When people sin their relationship with God is temporarily spoiled, but their relationship with God is certainly not broken. It is evident even from the marriage relationship that a husband may temporarily spoil his relationship with his wife in instances when he fails to be considerate, loving, or faithful. Restoring the spoiled relationship, as in the context of marriage, requires that the parties learn to say sorry. The husband does not need to get married all over again. It is the same with people's love relationship with God. By confessing their sins, turning away from what is wrong and trusting in His complete and absolute forgiveness, they can restore the spoiled relationship.

As Christians come closer to Jesus, the more faulty they will appear in their own eyes. Their vision will be clearer, and their imperfections will be seen in broad and distinct contrast to Christ's perfect nature. This recognition of one's sinfulness is evidence that a lasting relationship with God is in effect and that this self-reflection will be followed by deeper and more heartfelt confession and repentance.

Why Falling?

The work of Satan poses constant challenges for living a righteous life and is accountable for the fall of most strong and good Christians. The devil aims to make all people sin. In several points the devil tempts all people to disown their faith or sin against their God and Creator. Life as a Christian is thus a battle and a march.

As free moral agents, we are all free to choose whom we will serve. Whether to expel sin or to remain in sin is the decision of an individual soul. "The strongest temptation is no excuse for sin. However great the pressure brought to bear upon the soul, transgression is our own act. It is not in the power of earth or hell to compel anyone to sin. The will must consent, the heart must yield, or passion cannot overbear reason, nor iniquity triumph over righteousness" (*Signs of the Times*, vol. 1, p. 379). We may not have the power to set ourselves free, but when we cry for help, Christ's power will achieve the expulsion of sin for us. We cannot continue to sin against our will if we call on Christ. People are thus responsible for their sins and their continued living in sin. Every temptation and test, every negative influence, whether open or secret, may be successfully resisted "not by might nor by power" but by the Spirit of the Lord (Zech. 4:6). Sin is never a matter of necessity but of choice.

God's Reaction to Sinning

You may be asking the question, how does a merciful God take it when His children fall into sin? God is stern to those who continue in sin (see Rom. 11:22). God's rejection of the chosen nation Israel when they continued in sin serves as a warning of God's decisiveness on sin and sinners. Ancient Israel's persistent unbelief led God to reject them as a special people. Therefore, "If God did not spare the natural branches, he will not spare you either" if you continue in sin (Rom. 11:21).

God by His very nature hates sin and does not excuse sin, irrespective of its perceived magnitude. God does not vindicate our falling or sinning no matter how small the transgression or deviation may seem to us or how insignificant the circumstances seem that led to it. Falling into sin, whatever the cause, is not excusable and justifiable to God.

If we continue in sin, we sour our right relationship with Him and automatically exclude ourselves from His kingdom. Habitual sinners cannot enjoy the perfection that pervades heaven, and its beauty would be constant torment to them. God deals decisively and seriously with the people who *continue* in sin.

However, even though God hates sin, He loves the sinner. God does not cast off those overcome by the enemy or forsake or reject them if they sin. He extends His grace to all and invites them to forsake their evil ways. God receives all people who fall into sin if they come back to Him through true repentance. Christ is ready to intercede for us (see 1 John 2:1). If we repent and wholeheartedly call on Him, he forgives us. There is no reason for despair and hopelessness.

> ## Two Reactions to Falling
>
> Two reactions are possible after falling into sin. The first involves discouragement and abandoning all efforts to restore one's (good) standing with God. This is a big problem, for a person taking that approach remains fallen. The second involves taking our fall as a springboard to have a fresh attempt at having a right relationship with God. Under this, second, response, the sinners' view of their own sinfulness drives them to Christ instead of repelling them from Him.
>
> In actual fact the difference between those who are going to be saved and those who are going to be lost is not that the latter never fell into sin, but that they rose whenever they fell. Thus, what is pertinent is what a person does after he or she has fallen. We need to repent of our sin without being overcome with discouragement at our failure or beginning to doubt God's love.

The fact that people fall and that they cannot stop sinning even with the mind in the right place means that our salvation depends not on what we have done but on what God is doing for us. We are saved not on our merit but rather by grace. This truth quickly becomes evident and essential because clearly all people fall. The reality and import of the fact that we fall should drive Christians to humility and a more decided, acute sense of their need for mercy.

> ### Sinning Has Consequences
> Many take God for granted thinking that because God's grace is so abundant why not sin all the more? Christians need to be aware that though God forgives sin, He does not prevent its consequences from taking their course (see Exod. 34:7). When people sin the consequences of their sins come to them even when God forgave them. In the case of David, his sin led to the death of four of his sons, caused a civil war, and weakened the moral fiber of the nation. Each person who sins reaps a harvest. The results of sin, no matter how small, are long-lasting and bitter.

Overcoming falling

Ty Gibson explained that to succeed as a Christian and minimize falling and sinning, Christians need to maintain a consciousness of two realities: (1) God is powerful enough to keep us from falling. All Christians need divine power and assistance to resist the devil and aid their efforts. God provides sufficient grace and sufficient power to keep all from falling. To access this power, Christians need to be in constant submission to the will of God and be totally dependant on Him; otherwise, they will surely fall. All heaven, with its limitless resources, is placed on the command of each soul that depends on God. (2) As we move heavenward, mercy is immediately exercised toward us if we fall. By the grace of God, men and women of God can gain fresh vigor to once again rise from their fall and rise above their evil natures. When we come to Christ, He will pardon and transform our lives and restore a positive relationship with Him. Every mortal being has access to God's mercy.

Whenever we fall, God wants to restore us to the right relationship with Himself. Falling should not be the end in itself but always the beginning of a new victorious life and experience in Christ.

More importantly, Christians need to be clothed with Christ's righteousness to be victors. Christians need to lay hold on Christ in order to subdue every sinful trait they may have and resist every temptation that may come their way. Constantly reach out to God in continual and earnest repentance.

Chapter Fourteen

Looking at the Prize

An athlete is not crowned unless he competes according to the rules—2 Timothy 2:5, ESV

Developing a lasting relationship with God is not futile; it will be highly recompensed. The process may entail cost, but as Jesus promised, the prize for running in the race shall be far greater than the cost. It is no vain thing to serve God, to be His disciple, to obey and fear Him, or to fight evil, for He shall truly recompense all. Jesus said, "No one who has left home or wife or brothers or parents or children for the sake of the kingdom of God will fail to receive many times as much in this age and, in the age to come, eternal life" (Luke 18:29, 30). All faithful Christians will receive their reward for entering and maintaining a lasting relationship with God.

Many people have different ideas as to what exactly constitutes the prize that God has in store for faithful Christians. Many people fancy the prize as consisting of "hardware" rather than "software." Their imaginations are drawn (and limited) to things they can touch and see—the streets of gold, the pearly gates, the beautiful trees, the river of life in heaven, and the crown of life, among other things. It is these tangible things—the "hardware"—that people tend to associate with the prize. True, the faithful

Looking at the Prize

Christians are going to enter the courts of heaven and walk on the streets of gold and eat of the tree of life. It is, however, pertinent to note that a closer look at Scripture shows that this almost temporal view of the prize is not only incomplete but misses its real and fundamental essence.

The essence of the prize consists of the more fulfilling and deeply enriching "software," the perfect, cordial, and uninterrupted relationship and fellowship that people are going to have with God. The prize is primarily to be viewed in terms of the quality and nature of the relationship Christians are going to enjoy with God (undisturbed and perpetual) and with the other saints, the absence of sin and sinners, and the restored nature and being of humankind. The prize consists in the restoration of people's perfect relationship with God. This is why the author of Revelation, in addition to revealing the physical features of heaven, spends a lot of time describing the special, renewed, and positive relationship that will characterize the life in heaven. People will be restored to the original state enjoyed at Creation, the enjoyment of perfect communion and loving relationship with God.

In heaven, the saved "shall always be with the Lord" (1 Thess. 4:17, NKJV). Revelation 21 describes some of the blessings of their consummated reunion with God in heaven. They will enjoy the society of angels and communion with God and His son. Their powers will be elevated and extended throughout eternal ages. As part of the prize, they will sit on the same throne with God (see Rev. 3:21). In heaven the dwelling of God will be with people, and God Himself will live with them (see Rev. 21:3). Thus salvation is a relationship and not just a business transaction.

The enjoyment of a perfect, cordial, and lasting relationship with God is the ultimate prize for Christians, and enjoying the infrastructure in heaven is part of the package. Once saved, Christians will also, walk on streets of gold, eat from the tree of life, and sit by the river, to name only a few of the enjoyments in heaven. Describing both the hardware and software components of heaven, Paul says, "No eye has seen, no ear has heard, no mind has conceived what God has prepared for those who love him" (1 Cor. 2:9).

None of us has ever fully understood the value of what God has prepared for His people. He has prepared something that is new, different, and better than anything we have seen, felt, and known. Even in our wildest imagination, we cannot even come close to conceiving the joy that awaits us in heaven. In heaven God has prepared everything we love. We will live in peace and experience true joy and happiness. God has more than enough to thrill every person for eternity. We will worship God and thank Him for His mercies. Our brains will be energized and our senses sharpened. All people will reach the lofty heights God created them to attain. Old sinful pasts will not be remembered there. Importantly, in heaven we will be reunited with our loved ones who have died. Personally, I will be ecstatic to meet my grandmother, whom I loved so much, and my lovely sister, Retina who passed away in 2011. It will be thrilling to meet and talk with Moses,

Abraham, Joshua, Gideon, David, Solomon, just to name a few of my heroes.

The non-existence of sin and its associated results will make life pleasurable in the city of God. A world and life with no death, no mourning, no crying, no pain, where people will never go hungry or thirsty, is indeed a reward to look forward to. As Robert Folkenberg observed, a world simply devoid of all the negatives that currently define fallen life on earth "would be wonderful even if its streets weren't paved with gold or its gates weren't made of pearl."[10] In heaven people's relationship with other perfect humans will be cordial, perfect, and mutual.

Understanding the heavenly prize as being primarily relational enables us to grasp why evildoers are unfit for heaven and will not be permitted to enter its gates. Individuals who have refused to be reconciled with God in this life would shrink away in disgust if they were to be allowed into heaven. Evil people cannot and would not relate with God in His unveiled glory. They would prefer and welcome destruction rather than face Him and live with Him for eternity. If people refuse or fail to enter into and maintain a right relationship with God in this life, they render themselves unfit for life in heaven.

Reward is a Gift

It is important to note that people cannot claim the reward that God offers on merit. It is only through the unmerited grace of Christ that any person can be saved. We need Christ's righteousness to get to heaven. Christians are saved by grace but this

(cont.)

> grace must be accepted if a person is to be saved. God respects people's choices. Only those who have accepted His offer of salvation will be allowed into His kingdom.

When Jesus comes the second time, He is going to reward each person according to what he has done (see Matt. 16:27; Rev. 22:12). The reward is based on what each person would have done in this life. Before God grants all people their prizes or rewards, they ought first to pass through the process of judgement. The Bible says that prior to the second coming of Jesus, when Jesus will return to grant people their rewards, the heavenly courts shall sit with Jesus, who is the judge, to consider the cases of all the living and the dead (see Eccl. 12:13, 14; 2 Cor. 5:10). Each case will be carefully considered and will be decided for good or for evil.

According to theologian Dr. Jon Paulien, there is only one issue that matters in the judgment: "what think ye of Christ?" One's relation to (or posture toward) Christ is what matters. Numerous Bible passages confirm this view (see Matt. 18:21–25, 25:40, 45; John 12:48, 15:23). Clearly, Christ will judge us by *our accountability to God and to others.* Those who reject God or refuse to be accountable to Him in this life stand condemned before God. It is as simple as that. Whoever believes in Jesus is not condemned, but whoever does not believe stands condemned.

God in the judgement does not weigh the good deeds vis-à-vis the evil deeds in a bid to find out on which side of the scale one's deeds will tilt. The judgement process is the heavenly chosen procedure to confirm whether the people truly had a lasting and positive relationship with God in their lives. God is interested in ascertaining a simple fact: whether an individual had and maintained a positive relationship with Christ during his or her life on earth. Those who had a lasting relationship with Him will be rewarded, and those who did not will not be rewarded.

The judgement process does not change anything but merely confirms what people themselves have chosen in their lives. It is not judgment but character that determines destiny. When our characters are in line with our professed relationship with God, judgment simply confirms it. The people who choose to have a relationship with Christ in this life will be ushered into heaven. People who are living their lives for Christ and with Christ, carefully and constantly developing their relationship with Him, need not fear judgment. They need to approach judgment with a smile and expect nothing but a good prize.

The distinction between those who have a positive relationship with God and those who do not is so marked to God that separating the two is like separating goats from sheep.

Those who have rejected God's invitations for reconciliation through Christ on this earth have sown the corruptible and from that nature will reap corruption. Their rejection of God and their continuation in sin have unfitted them for friendship with Him and ultimately eternal life in heaven. The Bible says that those who rejected Him have been condemned already (see John 3:18). It is impossible to enter heaven when one has refused to accept and acknowledge God as Father and King. The same fate awaits the many who start a relationship with God but do not follow through in their commitment to God, even through their names may remain in the church books.

The only people who are going to stand during God's judgements are those who would be clothed with the righteousness of Christ. They would have repented of and forsaken their sins. They would have allowed God to mould their characters after His will. Enoch had such a developed and positive relationship with God that God found it necessary to take him to heaven before he tasted death. Enoch lived his life on earth as in the presence of God. His character was Christlike, and he enjoyed a lasting and well-developed relationship with God. The Bible says Enoch walked with God. God is seeking for people like Enoch, who, though living in an evil environment, maintain a close walk with God.

The reward in heaven is a significant incentive and encouragement to all Christians to motivate them to work on their relationship with God more decidedly. The existence and assurance of the prize should keep all Christians focused in their quest to cultivate, develop, and maintain a lasting relationship with God in this life. The secret for Moses in Egypt was that he was looking at the prize ahead. Scriptures say that he chose rather to be ill-treated along with the people of God because he was looking to the future at the reward. It is because of the promise of a prize that consecrated Christians endure trial and temptations for Christ's sake, are steadfast in the war with evil, and serve God. The promise and understanding of what God has prepared for those who love Him propel Christians to action. With no reward to look forward to, Christianity becomes meaningless.

Soon we shall see our redeemer and Savior in all His glory face to face. How we will rejoice on that blessed day when His glory shall be seen! What a blissful moment it shall be when we behold and meet our Savior and Lord nevermore to part.

Now as probation lingers, it is time for you to put away and correct the deformities in your character and fit yourself for heaven. May God be your help so that you may, like Martin Luther holding fast God's Word against the emperor and Pope, declaring, "Here I take my stand; I cannot do otherwise. God be my help."

---

10   Folkenberg, p. 30.

We invite you to view the complete
selection of titles we publish at:

www.TEACHServices.com

Scan with your mobile
device to go directly
to our website.

Please write or email us your praises, reactions, or
thoughts about this or any other book we publish at:

TEACH Services, Inc.
P U B L I S H I N G

www.TEACHServices.com

P.O. Box 954
Ringgold, GA 30736

info@TEACHServices.com

TEACH Services, Inc., titles may be purchased in bulk for
educational, business, fund-raising, or sales promotional use.
For information, please e-mail:

BulkSales@TEACHServices.com

Finally, if you are interested in seeing
your own book in print, please contact us at

publishing@TEACHServices.com

We would be happy to review your manuscript for free.

CPSIA information can be obtained at www.ICGtesting.com
Printed in the USA
BVOW031458141212

307891BV00001B/3/P